PRAISE FOR "THE QUALIFIED SALES LEADER"

John McMahon has just about single-handedly changed the way enterprise technology companies sell. As an executive, board member, advisor, and investor, John has not only coached a generation of companies on selling, but he has also influenced a generation of technology executives and investors. I have learned as much from John McMahon about selling, business, and leadership as I have from any other person on the planet. Drop what you are doing and read **The Qualified Sales Leader** right away.

Mike Speiser-Managing Director-Sutter Hill Ventures

John McMahon is the G.O.A.T. of enterprise software sales. Few writers have been able to simplify the key aspects of enterprise software sales as John has accomplished in The Qualified Sales Leader. **The basics of sales leadership are combined with the essentials to guide reps through the customer journey, maximizing customer business value and sales order value.** Any rep or leader who is looking to succeed in enterprise sales should read this book. I highly recommend it.

John Kaplan-Co-Founder of Force Management

Most sales books are boring, clinical "textbooks" that "cookie-cutter" a few generic ideas into a monotonous, dull read, that puts you to sleep. ***The Qualified Sales Leader is an easy read, dripping with the fundamentals of enterprise sales. Real world advice that you'll put to use the next day.***

Chris Degnan-CRO-Snowflake

The Qualified Sales Leader is an easy to read conversational and narrative style book that will absolutely resonate through the halls of any enterprise software sales team. ***Realistic, usable advice for any sales leader or sales rep. If you're in enterprise sales, you'd be crazy not to read this book.***

Cedric Pech-CRO-MongoDB

It's been decades since the sales profession received a gift like this amazing book. It's based on the fundamentals that underpin how individuals and teams must operate in order to win in a consistent, predictable manner. These lessons are shared in the clear voice of software's winningest sales leader- John McMahon. **The Qualified Sales Leader** is a "must read" for anyone who is committed to the pursuit of excellence in sales leadership.

Carlos Delatorre, CRO-TripActions

John has positioned himself firmly in the enterprise sales hall of fame. *The learnings in* ***The Qualified Sales Leader will help you and your sales team sell more deals, make more money and grow your career in enterprise sales***. I'd highly recommend every sales leader and any sales reps wanting to be a sales leader, pick up a copy, now.

Luca Lazzaron-CRO-Sprinklr

John earned his scars through real life experience as a sales leader operating in multiple startup to IPO companies growing 100% annually. ***John's learnings are etched into this powerful book, The Qualified Sales Leader.*** Do yourself a favor, buy the book and learn incredible sales leadership lessons.

Andy Byron-President-Lacework

The Qualified Sales Leader is more than a straight talk book for people with a sales title. ***It should be read by many venture capitalists and first-time tech CEOs to give them an under-***

standing of their enterprise sales teams and unlocking the full potential of their sales engine.

Neeraj Agrawal-General Partner-Battery Ventures

After working with John for several years, I urged him to write a book so that others, including myself, could learn from him. ***Buy a copy of The Qualified Sales Leader for every sales leader in your company.*** You will be glad you did. My highest recommendation.

Bob Beauchamp-CEO BMC Software

I grew up in John McMahon's sales organization. His ideas and rigor live on inside HubSpot's own sales machine. John McMahon is the preeminent sales leader. ***Read The Qualified Sales Leader if you want to level-up your sales leadership chops.***

Brian Halligan-CEO-Hubspot

Due to the explosion of tech companies, there is a sales leadership abyss leaving many great companies floundering to sell to initial customers and scale the company toward the ultimate goal of an IPO. ***The secret sauce in The Qualified Sales Leader provides the key ingredients to allow many tech company sales leaders to succeed in enterprise sales. Buy a copy, now.***

Chad Peets-Managing Partner-Sutter Hill Ventures

I've been waiting for John McMahon to write this book. ***John's groundbreaking work has built up an entire generation of sales leaders, and it's not by accident - his methodology and drive to outcomes are exceptional.*** There are many sales books out there, but few provide the level of insights and practical advice that **The Qualified Sales Leader** does. I'm excited to put more of these lessons into practice with my team!

Dennis Lyandres-CRO Procore

I've been in software for twenty-six years, have been part of four IPOs, and worked with many top people in enterprise sales. John McMahon is the GOAT for Sales Leadership. Why do I say this? The sales leaders who built the teams at Datadog, MongoDB, Medallia, Okta, Qualtrics, AppDynamics, Sprinklr, Lacework, and many other unicorns were all hired, trained and led by John.

The Qualified Sales Leader is John's proven, repeatable play-book for building world-class sales teams. If you want to build teams like this then delve deep into this story; these are the answers to the test. Good Selling!!

Dan Fougere—CRO-Datadog

No one in the software industry has developed more world class leaders and enterprise salespeople than John. ***In this book you will learn practical ways to significantly increase your revenues, develop world class teams, and become a true great in enterprise sales.*** If that's what you want, buy **The Qualified Sales Leader** quickly.

Jeremy Duggan-Former VP-EMEA at AppDynamics and BMC

The Qualified Sales Leader simply shows how sales leaders can motivate their sales reps to drive business value for the customer and maximize sales performance for the rep during the customer journey. **Few books discuss the basics of sales leadership in terminology that can be applied immediately.** If you want to influence your SaaS sales team, buy the book now.

Jim Drill-Ex-CRO at Imperva, Lithium, IMLogic

Finally, a sales leadership book, simply written, and based on the basic fundamentals of enterprise sales. ***The Qualified Sales***

Leader is loaded with an arsenal of practical information for any sales leader, and most sales reps, to apply immediately. Don't hesitate. Get on Amazon and buy a copy now.

Adam Aarons-President-Classy, ex-CRO-Okta

I'd recommend The Qualified Sales Leader to anyone that wants to understand the enterprise sales process; startup CEO's, CRO's, VC's, private equity firms and certainly sales reps and sales leaders. An easy read on the foundational elements of maximizing sales while driving tangible value for the customer. Well done!

Bob Ranaldi-Senior Growth Advisor-FTV Capital

The Qualified Sales Leader

Non-fiction

Cover designed by Mothershed Design Company.

THE QUALIFIED SALES LEADER

PROVEN LESSONS FROM A FIVE-TIME CRO

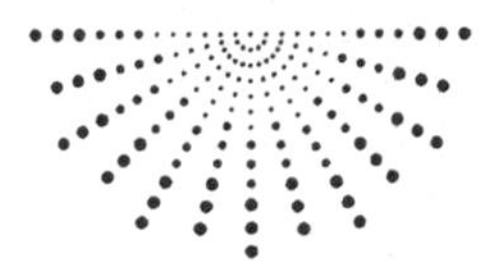

JOHN MCMAHON

Foreword by

DEV ITTYCHERIA

DEDICATION

To my father who taught me the incredible power of Ph.D. (Persistence, heart and Desire)

To all the incredible people with whom I've worked. As a "student of the game", I learned everything in this book from you. Thank you.

FOREWORD BY DEV ITTYCHERIA

CEO OF MONGODB

When I look back on my career, there are a handful of people who have made a profound impact on my professional life. John McMahon is one of them. It was the summer of 2005, and I was the co-founder & CEO of BladeLogic. We had started the company in August 2001 and raised our first round of venture capital financing five days before 9/11. At that time, the tech industry was already reeling from the dot com crash of 2000. It was a crazy time to start a new tech company, and somehow, through a lot of sweat, persistence, and luck, we managed to build a meaningful business that grew quickly, doubling year after year.

However, I had a pit in my stomach when I met with our chairman, Steve Walske, that summer. Steve had previously been the chairman & CEO of PTC. Those who follow the software industry know that PTC was one of the most successful software companies of the '90s, going from zero to $1.1B in revenue in just nine years, and, impressively, delivered forty-percent operating margins at the same time. PTC's sales team had a legendary reputation. Steve was not just chairman of our board;

he was also a mentor—someone whose advice and counsel I often sought out.

I shared with Steve that I wasn't feeling good about the state of our business. Our sales team was not firing on all cylinders. My confidence with our sales execution was waning, and I worried that the company would hit a wall if we had a couple of bad quarters as we were thinly capitalized. "If you want to know what a world-class sales leader looks like, go see John!" said Steve in his characteristically blunt style. John had been the head of sales at PTC. Our own sales team—several of whom had come from PTC—had previously mentioned John's name many times as someone they looked up to.

Intrigued, I phoned John, and I, along with my co-founder, met him for coffee in a hotel near our office outside of Boston. After that initial meeting, and a few other follow-up meetings, John accepted the offer to lead our sales organization. Later he would assume the role of COO. We took the company public two years after John joined, and, less than a year later, the company was acquired by BMC Software at the highest revenue multiple paid for a company in that period. None of this would have happened if John had not joined BladeLogic

To put things into perspective, John is the only person I know of that has been the head of sales for five different public software companies—PTC, Geo-Tel, Ariba, BladeLogic, and BMC. Moreover, thirty-three people and counting from BladeLogic's sales organization became Chief Revenue Officers (the modern title for a head of sales) for other software companies. Today, he is on the board of MongoDB, Snowflake, and a number of other noteworthy software companies. John has had an extraordinary impact on the software industry and is a legend in software sales.

Typically, most technology companies are founded by people with technical backgrounds, but who have limited experience in or knowledge of sales or sophisticated go-to-market strategies. Moreover, most venture capital and private equity investors have limited operational experience in sales. While they are good at pattern matching, every business has its own particular nuances, including customer buying behavior, deal size, sales cycle times, and competitive dynamics, so trying to pattern match from company to company can yield bad outcomes. Unfortunately, most founders and boards take sales for granted. They only focus on sales when the company is going to miss a number, but they don't spend sufficient time to understand whether a company is putting in the right foundational infrastructure for long term sales success.

As a result, most companies have a haphazard approach to sales. These companies do not know who their ideal customer profile is, let alone how to pursue them; are not clear on the type of salespeople they should hire; have not built a prescribed sales process with measurable steps; have no discernible qualification methodology to understand where a deal is or how much work is left to do; and do little to hold salespeople accountable to completing each step in the process, so they cut corners and end up with bad outcomes.

Building a sales organization is not easy, nor is it cheap, so it is one of the most daunting decisions for any company. Any leader, whether a CEO or a first-line manager, will at times struggle with sales. They'll wonder why the number was missed after rosy forecasts, whether the pipeline for the next quarter is as good as it seems, why some sales reps are successful, and why others, who have all the right attributes, are not. They'll try to discern how to keep their best salespeople when other companies are throwing a lot money at those same employees, and they'll wonder how they can scale their organization while delivering consistent results.

Like most people, I've found that bookstores are full of boring books written about sales leadership. These books leave the reader with a completely empty feeling. It's as if they took a college course in sales leadership taught by a professor with little to no actual experience in sales leadership. That's because most sales leadership books lack real-world, practical advice. If the author had sales leadership experience, it seems their knowledge was limited to a single experience in only one company, which lends to the application of a cookie-cutter solution to problems in all salesforces. Or they were sales consultants, who don't have real-world scars from living through the frustrating experiences of building multiple sales teams from the ground up. They never had to live with and learn from the implications and pains of bad decisions in building and managing a salesforce.

This book is designed for founders, CEOs, investors, business unit leaders, salespeople, and even engineers who want to understand what it takes to build a highly effective and impactful sales organization. Looking back, I believe one of the reasons John and I clicked well together is because both he and I studied engineering in college, so we both have a natural inclination to be analytical, to break down things into their piece parts. John applied this philosophy to sales, and he's done exactly that in The Qualified Sales Leader. And he has real-world experience, so the reader can immediately apply what they learn from the book into their business.

The Qualified Sales Leader is not a long book, but the quality of information is high. After more than twenty-five years working in tech, I found myself learning new things from this book. I believe other readers will do the same and enjoy their time doing so.

--Dev Ittycheria

Dev has experience as an entrepreneur, operator, and investor. He founded two companies, led and scaled multiple software companies, and made personal and institutional investments in a number of other disruptive software companies. He is currently the CEO of MongoDB and a member of the board of directors at DataDog.

You call me a fool
You say it's a crazy scheme
This one's for real
I already bought the dream
So useless to ask me why
Throw a kiss and say goodbye
I'll make it this time
I'm ready to cross that fine line
--Steely Dan

PART I
THE QBR

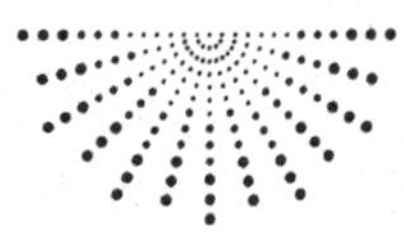

1

INTRODUCTION

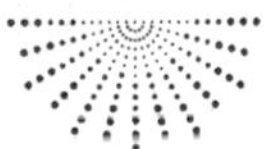

Will anyone be able to uncover the facts?

Every quarter, in almost every sales force, the same meeting takes place: the QBR a.k.a. the Quarterly Business Review.

I've run countless QBR's and have attended many more as an invitee for different software companies, and, in each one, the same interesting phenomenon occurs: a game is played out. A team of sales reps and managers convene in a conference room, and, one by one, they're called on to participate in a forecast-review session.

Each rep nervously stands in front of their manager and team members to review their forecast for the quarter. They're *totally* exposed. There's no place to hide. They knew this moment was inevitable. They knew they should have prepared to stand in front of their peers with complete confidence.

So, here they are, staring down the moment when their forecast will be judged by the entire sales force. The strength of their business pipeline will be revealed. Reality will be unveiled. The truth determined.

In a forecast review, reps often find it difficult to be completely honest about their account situations. They may have difficulty setting their pride and egos aside and viewing account situations without bias. Reps have a hard time learning from their managers' inquiring questions. Questions that may reveal a reality quite different from what the reps believe regarding their account scenarios. They struggle. But they need to learn.

Learning happens *in* the struggle.

For the QBR to be a learning session (as it should be), the sales reps need to accept that they aren't the only ones with account issues. They need to learn from mistakes—theirs as well as others'. For every rep who presents a specific account situation for the first time, there are other reps who have already experienced that situation. And still others who will see that same situation in the future.

Lessons shared become lessons learned.

The QBR should be utilized to coach reps and analyze their sales knowledge and sales skills. The manager-rep interaction shouldn't be a one-way interrogation. But, in many instances, that's how it evolves.

Due to time constraints and the number of people who will present, managers, using the power of position, impatiently hammer reps in a one-way inquisition without intending to guide or teach.

If the QBR is never leveraged as a way to capture account dynamics, understand buyer scenarios, learn about the competition, and discover ways to quantify customer value, the time is wasted. Eventually, reps will need to learn to self-analyze their account scenarios.

Unfortunately, that's not how the typical QBR runs.

Too often, reps are faced with massive pressure to present a forecast with a high likelihood of quota achievement. No rep wants to forecast less than quota for the quarter.

The QBR shines a white, hot spotlight on each rep's capability to build pipeline, qualify opportunities, and sell effectively. Even newer reps don't want to stand in front of their peers and say, "I don't have any deals that will close this quarter."

Who would?

For that reason, many reps stretch the truth in their forecast presentation. It's a Potemkin façade, designed to hide a truth that isn't quite as good as you would hope.

Some sales reps exaggerate and embellish deal scenarios and potential closing outcomes. Others may have had confirmation bias, or "happy ears," when they called on accounts. They heard what they wanted to hear and saw things through rose-colored glasses, believing certain accounts will close in the quarter, when in actuality they won't. They often present highly unlikely hopes and dreams of accounts closing within the remaining weeks of the quarter.

They'll need a bigger pillow for those dreams.

In an effort to sandbag their quarterly quota, a few reps have qualified deals properly but mask the true potential size of the deal and its probability to close.

The combination of "happy ears," rose-colored glasses, and sandbagging efforts forces managers to qualify the accuracy of forecasts by listening to fictional stories and searching for the truth in the forecasted opportunities.

That's why, when invited by the board of director of a struggling SaaS (Software as a Service) company named Forego to attend their QBR in New York City as a consultant, I was curious to learn whether or not Forego was similar to most.

The QBR occurred off site in a large conference room on the fifty-seventh floor of a building on 48th and Avenue of the Americas. As I walked into the conference room, I took in the amazing views of the Manhattan skyline with New Jersey sitting in the distance, across the Hudson River.

I found a seat next to the CRO and CEO and dropped my belongings. I was early, so I walked around to introduce myself, greeted a number of familiar faces, and grabbed a coffee. After mingling, I sat down to watch as the final parade of sales reps and managers entered the room.

All of us waited for the spectacle to begin.

2
SHANNON

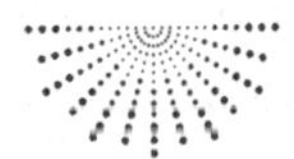

The CRO yelled, "OK, let's get started. Who's up first?"

The level of intensity rose in the room like an explosion from a gun. The mood changed from loud, casual talk about sports, weekends, and travel issues, to the stillness of a library at midnight. Only the shuffling of feet and movement of chairs, as people took their seats, could be heard.

Wow, I thought as a visceral tension grew as if someone had sucked the air out of the room. Facial expressions stiffened, and body language changed. Both experienced and inexperienced reps could likely feel the anxiety mounting in their guts.

Some reps look visibly shaken, I thought.

Like they need to take a deep breath to control their heart rates.

The first rep, a woman named Shannon, headed to the front of the room. Shannon had immigrated from Ireland several years prior, after leading a small, inside sales team. Now, she worked as an outside rep who called on larger-sized businesses.

One could easily be duped by Shannon if they weren't careful. She possessed a soft façade, but, on closer examination, she had a clear internal toughness, the kind that developed over hard knocks in life. It gave her an obvious edge that I could sense in her immediately—she was ready to handle whatever anyone threw at her.

Empathy for Shannon grew as other sales reps prepared to witness a pack of hyenas attacking weaker prey.

No one wanted to present first. Shannon had been the unlucky chosen one, or maybe she chose to go first to wash away the anxiety of waiting to present.

Presenting first meant the sales leaders were freshly caffeinated and not yet tired. Through the day, they would continue to fuel their minds and bodies with caffeine to heighten their senses, but in the morning, they were raw and ready to rumble.

The room wasn't intended to be intimidating, but the whole setup was daunting. A podium stood up front near two large screens, one on each side. From the podium, reps faced more than sixty people, including people representing the Sales, Presales, Post-Sales, and HR Departments.

Oh, and if that wasn't enough, the tribunal also attended—CEO, CFO, and CPO—which added unnecessary heat to an already-rising room temperature.

While Shannon made her way to the podium, the various sales managers seemed to prep their questions like Ginsu knives. They'd carve up her forecast and figure out the truth.

With her chin held high, Shannon presented her first deal. A bombardment of questions materialized from her manager, Andy, and Andy's manager, the area sales director.

"Who will approve this purchase?" Andy asked.

"My Champion told me that he has the budget," Shannon said confidently. "He told me I don't need to worry about it."

Andy let that go without further question.

She has a Champion or a coach?

Meanwhile, my palms grew sweaty. She started describing another unlikely deal in which one person controlled the entire buying process. She couldn't tell us about any other stakeholders. She simply said, "This is the way they make all technology purchases."

Other managers chimed in with other relentless, superficial questions:

- Why do you think you're going to get the deal?
- How long have you worked on this deal?
- When do you think the deal will come in?
- Do you think they'll buy this quarter?
- Who is the competitor?
- Is there anything you're worried about?

Superficial.

They never dug into the obvious red flags in her presentation.

In another deal, in which Shannon was selling to a large financial institution for the first time, she forecasted $250,000.

"There's no competition," she said. "They told me the deal is in their approval process but hasn't yet moved to procurement."

No competition?

"When was your latest update?" a manager asked.

"I haven't spoken with my Champion about it in a few days," Shannon said.

"Any word from legal over whether their lawyers have redlined anything yet?"

Shannon swallowed hard. "I haven't checked."

The managers were excited about this prospective deal, because it would be their first deal into a large NYC financial-services company. In their excitement, they glossed over serious issues.

I felt uncomfortable and shifted in my chair.

Does the customer know they will be buying $250,000 of software this quarter?

No one thought it could be an issue that Shannon hadn't spoken to her Champion recently.

No one raised a flag that a $250,000 deal with a new vendor, inside a large financial institution, hadn't caught the attention of the competition. They assumed that it would sail through the Legal and Procurement Departments without a protracted pricing negotiation.

The fourth deal she forecasted was deep into the last stage of the sales process, but the buyer had stopped responding to Shannon's calls.

"Why does the customer need the software?" one of the managers asked.

"I have a fantastic relationship with them, so I'm not that worried about it. We haven't spoken in ten days, but it will be fine. A lot of personal things must have happened, and they're probably just dealing with them."

Hasn't spoken to her Champion in ten days?

The managers didn't seem to notice her lack of answer to their question. I doubted whether Shannon even knew *why* this buyer needed to purchase.

On another deal, Shannon said, "I spoke with my Champion last night. They like the product but think it's too expensive. He wants a seventy-percent discount."

"That would significantly decrease your original forecasted deal size from $100,000 to $30,000," Andy pointed out. "Why are they demanding such a gigantic discount?"

Shannon shrugged. "Budgets are being cut. That's all the customers can afford at this time."

Really?

One manager glanced up from his computer. "There was a Nature Foods deal in the CRM system yesterday, but it's no longer on your forecast. Why?"

"The customer went through the testing process of our software and decided not to buy. At least we didn't lose to the competition. Just a lack of decision on their part."

No decision?

Interesting.

At that point, Andy and the managers succumbed to their own reality—they had exhausted all their questions and still didn't know which of her deals could close in the quarter.

There was this eerie feeling of confusion in the air. What number should they forecast? I had the uncomfortable feeling that no one knew the answer. Not Shannon, Andy, nor anyone else in the room.

But Andy asked the million-dollar question anyway. "How much are you going to forecast for this quarter?"

Understanding the criticality of the moment, and with a keen sense of what the right answer needed to be, Shannon gave her answer, "I forecast $250,000. With a shot for $300,000."

Shannon had enough experience to know that she needed to keep her forecast close to her $300,000 quota for the quarter. She made a safe—albeit not likely—choice. She wouldn't be annihilated for forecasting $250,000. But by adding, "with a shot to do $300,000," Shannon gave the management team what they wanted—hope of the possibility that she'd make her quarterly quota.

If her final number at the end of the quarter was $300,000, she'd look like a hero. If her final number at the end of the quarter was $200,000, she was still safe from manager repercussions. She could claim one deal slipped, making it seem that she wasn't far off from her forecast of $250,000.

Shannon walked away from the cross examination with her chin in the air.

3
CARLOS

Carlos was a hard-charging, ex-college-football player from Philadelphia, who had a jovial, like-able style. His presence said he wasn't a guy one could easily move in a mental or physical contest. When he took Shannon's spot on the podium, I hoped the best for him.

Andy seemed a little agitated, ready for his next interrogation. "Let's get it right out of the bag, Carlos. Cut to the chase. How much are you going to forecast for this quarter?"

"My number is $175,000," Carlos said confidently.

Andy's brow rose. "That's it? That's lower than your $300,000 quota. You know you can do better."

"I'm standing firm at $175,000."

The verbal beating commenced when another manager called out, "You're sandbagging your number."

"Nope," Carlos said. "That's what I'm comfortable forecasting. There's an upside deal from a large technology-services company that could push me to $250,000, but I'm not sure what the timeframe is for the approval and legal process. I don't know for certain, so I won't forecast that. I'll stick with $175,000."

They grilled him more, but Carlos seemed in control of his deals. He knew the customer environment, described their pains, understood the quantification of those pains, and knew how not solving the pain would have a negative effect on the customer's business. He'd clearly helped the customer develop the buying criteria in every deal.

He even knew what he didn't know—the signature process at the large tech-services institution.

This was one rep I admired. He dug in his heels. He wouldn't be peer-pressured into forecasting a higher number.

Sometimes reps sandbag. Sometimes the managers bully them into forecasting a higher number. Reps often want to forecast a lower number but end up succumbing to the pressure from their manager of forecasting a higher number. During the last week of the quarter, with no qualified deal to make up the difference, the reps drop their forecast to the lower number anyway. Then, their managers scramble to deal with the disparity.

"Then this is it," Andy said. "Final forecast. Will you be a team player and commit to the $300,000 that I know you can do, Carlos?"

Carlos stared at him, unwavering, and wiped away a bead of sweat over his bald head. He stood in a pool of pain, mumbled something underneath his breath in a clear internal argument with himself.

Would he give into the pressure or hold his ground?

"My forecast is $175,000," he said.

Andy shook his head. “We expected more of you.”

How will Andy make up the difference?

4
KATHLEEN

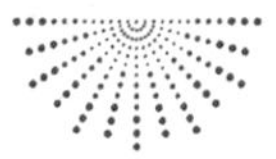

Kathleen stepped up to the podium next. Once she took her place between the screens, her manager, Jim, was ready. People easily took a liking to Jim. He had an aura and demeanor that spoke of natural leadership.

"Good morning, Kathleen."

She returned a Cheshire-Cat smile. "Good morning, Jim."

Her bubbly personality came through even in a situation as intense as the QBR. Kathleen was a former Division-I lacrosse player at Duke, where she'd set school records. She could also run like a gazelle, setting state records in the 200 meters and 400 meters. All on top of a 4.0 academic record.

This woman embodied competition.

"What's your forecast this quarter?" Jim asked.

"$350,000."

A little murmur ran through the room. I perked up, startled at her immediate confidence. Her over-quota forecast seemed to drive a different tone from Jim and the managers. Next to me, the CEO, Raj, leaned forward.

A sense of ease followed as Jim continued his questions.

"I met with my Champion's manager at Aramark last week," she said with a bright tone. "I believe that we can close this deal during this quarter."

"Why does the customer have to buy so quickly?" Jim asked.

"They raved so much about the latest feature release that we ended up having an hour-long discussion, which revealed their eagerness. I'm confident it can close in this quarter."

Kathleen had keenly avoided the question by discussing a random product feature set, but Jim didn't seem to notice. He moved on to the next account, McCormick.

"I've only called on McCormick once," Kathleen continued as she shuffled her feet behind the podium, "but they just asked for a proof of concept (POC). I believe that's indicative of their interest. Really, I think they're motivated enough, and they researched our product, because they defined their POC criteria and gave me a copy."

"How much is McCormick?"

"$50,000," Kathleen said.

"And your next deal?" Jim asked.

I frowned. The criteria were defined *before* Kathleen arrived.

"In my next account, Air Products, I've seen a competitive rep in the lobby, so I have a few mild concerns. I don't know to whom they're speaking within the company. My only contact is my Champion, but they told me not to worry."

Andy spoke up. "Kathleen, your Champion obviously isn't the only person involved. Who are the other account decision makers?"

"My Champion told me not to worry."

Andy countered, "But what if the competition is calling higher in the account?"

Kathleen shrugged.

No more probing questions?

Disastrous.

"What's your final deal?" Jim asked.

A suspicion crawled up the back of my spine. It seemed as if Jim heard what he wanted to hear from the beginning with Kathleen, because his interrogating backed off. He believed more about her account descriptions and deal statuses than he had with any of the other reps. Maybe he was giving Kathleen the benefit of the doubt because she forecasted above goal.

Maybe Kathleen had a good strategy: forecast above goal and the managers will go easy on you. Seemed like a backhanded signal to the other reps in the room to forecast above their number each quarter.

That spelled trouble for accurate forecasting.

Certainly, forecasting above their number every quarter is where every rep *wants* to find themselves, but managers have the historical performance data. Constantly forecasting above your number without any history of consistently closing above quota is asking for repercussions.

In the final deal Kathleen described, Andy jumped at his chance to raise a flag.

"You're forecasting Thompson again?" he said. "How many times will you forecast this deal? You called it two quarters ago for $200,000, last quarter for $100,000, and now you're forecasting $50,000. C'mon, Jim. You know this deal isn't real. It's been on the forecast for nine months. Take it off the forecast, already."

Kathleen smiled back at Andy.

I'd seen this in many deals before. Quarter after quarter, the deal size diminishes, slips into the next quarter, and then eventually disappears. It's a common tactic for a rep to keep presenting it. It's a forecast filler.

If the managers bought the story Kathleen had told for the last three quarters, why would she drop it from the forecast?

Thompson wouldn't close. It would evaporate next quarter, and Kathleen would avoid discussing it.

Time kills all deals.

All bad deals die a slow death.

Of course, Andy wasn't going to let her off easily.

"Jim, you aren't holding her accountable," Andy said. "She consistently finishes below forecast. Kathleen, you committed the Honeywell deal last quarter for $150,000. That slipped off the forecast the last few days of the quarter. Now, you're still including the slipped Honeywell deal in this quarter's forecast, which means your real forecast is only $200,000. Jim, you should hold her accountable to $450,000 this quarter. Her $300,000 quota and the slip deal for $150,000."

Jim let out a long breath, faced with the reality of not knowing the exact status of each deal. Which of Kathleen's deals would close in the quarter? It was almost impossible to say.

Jim ran a hand through his hair, his voice edged with frustration when he asked, “OK, how much are you going to forecast?”

“I forecast $350,000.”

She’ll need to pull a rabbit out of her hat.

Andy rolled his eyes as Kathleen walked away from the podium.

5
HANNLIN

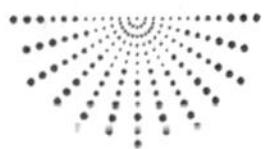

My head had started to ache from all the back-and-forth when the next rep took center stage.

Hannlin, was a tall, well balanced Texan from Houston. He had a chip on both of his shoulders. He lived with the need to prove . . . *something*. His family had a long heritage in the oil and gas industry, but Hannlin—against his father's approval—chose to blaze a path as a sales rep. That path required him to prove tangible success in the face of his father's intense scrutiny.

You're going to be a sales rep? I could imagine his father asking. *You'll end up bartending or waiting tables at a local Houston restaurant.*

Hannlin had only been with the company for six months when he stepped up to the podium and said, "I'm forecasting $400,000 this quarter. There are eight deals, all from new customers."

My ears perked up.

Hannlin was an activity machine, smothering accounts to ensure that he beat his goal. Despite his raw energy and drive, he was still inexperienced and naive—he had yet to close a single deal.

Eight new deals and they're all going to close?

Not likely.

When none of the managers asked how it was possible that a new rep would close eight new deals, I felt my stomach acid building.

Who would help him manage such a high level of activity?

"I just responded to an RFP (Request for Proposal) for HEB," he said. His body bobbed slightly, as if he stood on his toes. "I haven't called on the account yet, but after reviewing the RFP, I think it's a deal we can count on. There doesn't seem to be a one-hundred-percent direct match to our product, but I'll figure that out. They want to buy this quarter, so I'll capitalize on their urgency."

Good luck.

When Hannlin mentioned a second deal at Marathon, where he'd responded to an RFP who'd demanded the attachment of a price quotation, none of the managers attempted to calm his enthusiasm.

Cannon fodder.

Then Hannlin presented another deal at Cheniere, in which he'd performed a POC. "The customer told me I had won the proof of concept, but he wants me to run it again. He also told me to 'sharpen my pencil' on the price quote."

Run the POC again?

"Why do they want a lower price?" Jim asked.

Hannlin sucked in a sharp breath. "They just said that if I wanted to win the deal, I needed to 'sharpen my pencil.' Doesn't matter. I'm confident I can win the proof of concept again and get a purchase order before the end of the quarter. It may be a smaller-sized deal, though."

Hannlin was confident.

But not in control.

No requests for clarification came from the managers.

In another account, Hannlin was preparing to perform a proof of concept that week.

"My Champion showed me the final proof of concept criteria," he said, "but I'm concerned, because last week it changed. Some of our competition's key features are now in the criteria."

"What did your Champion say?" Jim asked.

"Said it's not a big deal. He still thinks I can win. So, I've forecasted it."

"But why would *you* win it?" Andy pressed. "If we don't have the key capabilities they added?"

"Because my Champion wants me to win."

Champion? Or coach?

Fed up, Andy asked about the elephant in the room, "If he wanted you to win, why were capabilities added that we don't have?"

"And, what about the $200,000 NTK deal you forecasted last quarter?" Jim asked from the sidelines.

"Ah, NTK." Hannlin shook his head. "My Champion told me the competition went over my head and met with the C-level people. After that meeting, we lost the deal."

Fascinating.

Hannlin discussed other accounts wherein customers wanted to run a proof of concept. But as he described his proof of concepts with the group, it became evident that he (and the entire sales force) ran them without any success criteria. Neither the customer nor the rep understood when the proof of concept was actually over.

Maybe the customer understood what they wanted to test, but the reps couldn't articulate why. And did the customers truly understand all the capabilities of the product? The reps were simply hoping the customers, after playing with the software, wanted to buy.

Customer—blind to product capabilities.

Rep—blind to customer needs.

Totally blind.

Is hope a good strategy?

I motioned to Jim with a raised hand. "How long does a typical proof of concept last?" I asked.

"On average," Jim said, "they last four weeks."

Four weeks without knowing if you're winning or losing? I thought.

No wonder this company desperately needs help.

"What is your POC win rate?" I asked.

"Twenty-five percent." A hint of color appeared in Jim's face, but he met my gaze. Only one-in-four customers that had performed a proof of concept had actually bought the software. Their average deal size was $50,000.

In the end, the managers let Hannlin stick with his forecast: $400,000

When pigs fly.

6

SAME SCENARIO, DIFFERENT REP

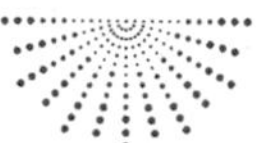

Throughout the forecast session, many words flew around: champion, coach, Economic Buyer, enemy, gatekeeper, recommender, technical buyer, user buyer, POC, demo, and justification.

But the context seemed inconsistent.

Reps spoke of account Champions, but were they really coaches? They discussed Champions without defining *why* they were Champions. They declared a meeting with an Economic Buyer. What made the person an Economic Buyer? Was anyone using the same definition for each term? Was there a common vocabulary amongst the sales force?

An entirely different story can be told when a group is using the same words . . . but with different meanings.

An agonizing notion occurred to me: the sales reps and the managers were talking past each other.

Not communicating.

Same words, different definitions. This resulted in different pictures of the actual account status and left them unable to find common ground on the next logical step.

As the day progressed, the game played on.

The caffeine buzz waned as the coffee turned cold and catered food ran thin. The managers tired and asked fewer grilling questions. Some reps slid by with little intensity from the managers. Their repeated, superficial questions lost their original punch and potency.

The tense environment eased in the room as well. The nervousness of the presenting reps decreased. Reps in the audience lost attention and even empathy for the remaining presenters. A few opened their laptops to check email and their social-media accounts.

The remaining reps gave what they believed to be the status of their deals, and the managers let red flags fly with so many unanswered questions. The managers asked questions on the periphery, never focusing on core account issues.

Never digging into the heart of the matter.

There was a common theme on each deal. Neither the rep nor the managers could articulate the exact stage of every deal, the exact status, nor the logical next step.

I had several questions in mind:

- Did they have a coach or a Champion?
- What information did they lack?
- Why did the customer have to buy?
- Who had final budget approval?
- Who controlled the deal?
- What is the urgency to buy?

- How will the customer justify the purchase?
- What is the customer's evaluation process?
- Were they winning or losing?
- Were they in control?

The management team tried to portray a sense of control over the forecast session, but they had none. In each rep session, after all their questioning, the back-and-forth, and the high anxiety, the result was to ask the rep for the answer: how much are you going to forecast?

In the meantime, the reps didn't learn to become better salespeople or better qualifiers. The reps didn't feel like they'd been heard. They felt like they were being used. Used for the showmanship of the managers. Used by the managers to commit to an unrealistic forecast number.

And the managers didn't garner any new information to help them forecast accurately or to coach their reps more effectively. The only thing that changed throughout the day was the intensity level of the questions.

What an ineffective way to manage a forecast session.

Dumpster fire.

7
THE ROLL UP

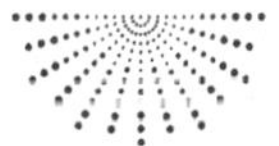

After all the reps presented, the feeling of relief in the room was nearly tangible. All the reps dispersed for a much needed coffee break and an opportunity to trade stories from the forecast session.

In a corner of the conference room, the managers and their bosses (the directors and VPs), gathered to tally up their forecasts. Shockingly, the results were unclear.

Even though they'd spent all day reviewing each and every deal, they still couldn't agree on what number to forecast. This led to another game—this time between the managers and directors.

Minor arguments arose between the managers and their directors regarding how much to forecast for each rep. After volleying back and forth, some rep's forecasts were lowered, and others were raised committing the managers to a number for the quarter.

Some managers tried to taint their reps' forecasts and tarnish their reps selling abilities in an effort to sandbag their own number while their directors tried to bully them into committing to a higher number. But, the managers knew they and their reps were poor forecasters and lacked a method to accurately qualify accounts, so better to be conservative and commit to a lower number.

Forecast low and finish high was the prevailing mindset.

Other managers remained completely quiet, no doubt considering the number their directors would ask them to commit to—and own—for the quarter.

Like a game of musical chairs, no one wanted to look *too* anxious about getting a chair (or nailing down a forecast number) until the last possible moment.

In the end, each manager committed to a number. Then *their* directors and VPs' committed to a number. The forecast rolled up to the CRO, who put his own spin on the forecast to the CEO, who committed the final number to the board of directors.

Now, they all had their reputations on the line.

Foam the runway.

8

MEETING WITH THE CEO

Eleven weeks passed by, and Forego's QBR left my mind. I'd seen many forecast session debacles before, so what occurred at Forego didn't seem all that surprising.

Then I got a phone call.

"John," said a crisp voice. "It's Raj from Forego. I need your help. You saw my QBR at the beginning of the quarter. I need you to help advise my sales force on how to sell accounts more effectively. I want the people on my sales force to be become better salespeople and better forecasters."

Right away, I recognized him. Not only his voice, but the sense of urgency behind his words.

"Raj," I said. "Good to hear from you. How did your quarter end?"

He scoffed. "Terribly. John, you watched my sales team during the QBR and my sales management team as they rolled up the forecast, which met our plan number. They seemed confident in their forecasting abilities. Unfortunately, we fell far short of the company plan."

No real surprise there.

The session had lacked any form of structure or methodology to establish forecast accuracy. His managers instinctively knew they lacked *line of sight to the number*. They'd had a moment of insanity or reckless courage, thrown caution to the wind, and forecasted the quarterly plan number. Maybe because they'd known what Raj wanted to hear but the managers had fallen far short of their forecast.

"How did some of the reps finish?"

"Shannon only closed $150,000, although she forecasted $250,000, with a potential for $300,000. Carlos jumped his forecast by $75,000 and closed $250,000 instead of $175,000. Kathleen, who forecasted to close $350,000 quota, wound up at only $150,000. The Thompson deal from the prior quarter slipped again. Hannlin, who forecasted $400,000, came in just shy of $50,000, closing only two of the eight deals he forecasted. No one seems to know how to forecast. No one is in control of their deals."

That's an understatement.

Certainly, that was a rough distinction between forecast and reality. Raj was a first-time CEO. Despite being a super-intelligent technologist, Raj was learning the ropes as the operator of a SaaS company.

But he knew what he didn't know . . . sales.

Raj was born and raised in Mumbai. He'd attended the Indian Institute of Technology Bombay, where he'd earned a Master of Science degree in Computer Science. After graduation, he immigrated to the US with only a suitcase and $150. Once there, he found a job working for Google in Mountain View, California, but transferred to their New York City office in Chelsea for a promotion.

A few years later, he decided to start his own SaaS company, named Forego. He initially raised ten million dollars from Joe Veesey at Seed Round Ventures in Palo Alto, California. Later, Gina Growth at Startup Ventures in Boston, Massachusetts led a follow-on round, and one additional round gave Forego the distinction of a unicorn and a market cap over one billion dollars.

"I'm an engineer," he went on to say. "I'll never understand the art involved in a sale, but I know everything is a process. And there's a science to every process. And every step can be measured in order to understand and control a process. My sales leaders lack an understanding of process and measurement, which means they can't control their accounts."

"Raj, in the words of James Harrington," I began.

> *Measurement is the first step that leads to control and eventually to improvement.*
>
> *If you can't measure something, you can't understand it.*
>
> *If you can't understand it, you can't control it.*
>
> *If you can't control it, you can't improve it.*

"It's time for my company to understand how to gain control of deals using a sales process and find ways to constantly improve, John," said Raj.

Raj instinctively knew what so many CEOs, sales managers, and reps don't—a sales force needs to implement foundational methods and realize specific metrics before they can scale:

1. A measurable sales process
2. A means to analyze the sales process and effectiveness of the sales force
3. Consistency and repeatability in rep performance across the salesforce with:
4. An increasing average new deal size
5. An expanding up-sell deal size from existing customers
6. A measurable improvement in quarter-to-quarter average sales productivity

Raj knew that in order to scale, he'd have to give his sales force structure, so they could communicate and operate effectively as a unit.

Like a professional orchestra.

Music is codified around the world. The musical notes: A, B, C, D, E, F, and G represent the pitch and length of a sound, and those sounds are set in an arrangement for a composition. Those basic notes represent the fundamental structure of written music and allow for the understanding, playing, and analysis of music for the conductor and every musician in an orchestra.

Raj's sales force was like an orchestra playing music with no fundamental structure; nothing was codified, and nothing could be analyzed. So, his leaders had no understanding of what was going right, what was going wrong, or what to change.

Raj needed to codify his sales process, selling motions, and the analysis of sales issues into a systematic, structural arrangement.

Of course, I knew that was where I wanted to take him next, but I wanted to understand his level of awareness.

"What do you think is the cause of these issues?" I asked.

"We grew rapidly as a company, which caused an obvious knowledge and skill gap. The gap exists between what made a rep successful two years ago and what makes a rep successful now. Two years ago, we were a startup, selling small deals to low levels within accounts.

"This is very common, Raj. Your reps are activity machines, selling features and functions at a high rate and pace. Show up and throw up. Vending. Not selling. Their efforts brought you deals and got you to this point, but things changed."

"Yes, our product line has expanded, matured, and is competitively differentiated. Now, we're selling a platform of multiple software products, which are all tightly integrated."

"That's right Raj, your software platform appeals to a higher-level buyer. Your sales force needs to advance up market as well as move up within organizations if you're to sell to larger companies—where there are more experienced and sophisticated buyers that care about business value. You've shifted from a single-stakeholder sale in small companies to a multi-stakeholder, multi-level sale in large companies. From low-level product sales to high-level business sales."

"Agreed," he said with some relief.

"Your reps and managers need to learn how to speak to different buyers at different levels of organizations. They need to understand how to effectively message to each buying persona and specific use cases. They'll need to learn how to qualify different types of opportunities at multiple levels of larger accounts. What worked before isn't working now."

"Precisely."

The biggest issue Raj faced wasn't with a changing product or market. It was with his sales managers. The first-line sales leader has the most profound effect on the recruitment of reps *and* the overall success or failure of sales reps.

His first-line sales leaders were reps when Forego had a simple product and sold product features in small accounts to a single, low-level stakeholder. His managers had generated business off of sheer activity when they sold: making more calls, sending more emails and video links, connecting to more people on LinkedIn.

Now, that was the only way they knew to manage reps who were currently trying to sell a more complex product to a more sophisticated business buyer in large accounts.

His managers only wanted to drive and measure activity. If they wanted to be successful as a company, the *managers* had a list of things to change:

- Stop confusing activities with accomplishment.
- Stop pushing reps to rush through the sales process.
- Master the customer conversation with specific personas and use cases.
- Understand how to sell business value, using a repeatable process.
- Learn to qualify deal advancement issues in account situations.
- Coach reps on how to control an opportunity.
- Understand how to forecast accurately.

Raj stated the obvious. "If I can't get my managers to learn new ways and adapt appropriately," he said, "then they'll never be able to train and coach the reps on how to analyze deals and sell effectively."

I worried that Raj didn't know what "good" looked like.

Forego, like so many other startup SaaS companies, had a broken system from the beginning. From the ground up, no one in the company knew what good looked like. They didn't know what to change or how to change their current processes and methods. I thought back to the reps at the QBR.

"Is there any formal onboarding or ongoing development training for your sales force?" I asked.

"All we have is a two-day orientation for all new employees. We also host a formal two-day training for the reps after their first month, but it's all product training, no sales training."

"And managers?"

"There hasn't been any training for the managers."

No surprise there. Companies regularly spend millions of dollars training sales reps and little-to-nothing training their leaders.

"How does the current situation negatively affect you?" I asked.

"The major issue is that the average productivity of the sales force remains low. It's very expensive to hire new sales reps without any indication of an increase in sales productivity. Without the ability to hire new reps, the business can't scale. I'm constrained."

"Why do you think sales productivity is low?"

He laughed. "Well, first of all, we've never targeted the perfect customers for Forego. And we're poor qualifiers, so every account looks like a great prospect. Since we haven't identified our ideal targets and we can't qualify, we hang onto accounts that will never buy. That wastes time and lowers sales productivity."

Targeting the right customers with use cases that aligned to Forego's product differentiators, and then qualifying them once they were in the pipeline, would go a long way to salvage the situation.

He continued, "Our average deal sizes are small. The small deal sizes make it difficult for reps to meet their quotas and for the sales force to increase productivity. Only a small percentage of my sales reps are hitting their quota, so the majority aren't making money which is leading to attrition."

"Finally, to make matters worse, we're a subscription software company where customers need to annually renew their subscription, and many aren't renewing. So, our customer churn is too high. For every three deals my sales force brings in every quarter, we lose one. That's not sustainable."

He's skating on thin ice.

Forego's customer churn was high because they sold too low in companies for small dollars. Selling small deals at low levels in a company, without the customer understanding the tangible business value of the product, causes a high degree of customer churn. If a customer doesn't understand the business value of a subscription product, the customer won't renew their annual subscription.

Raj was also correct about forecasting. Accurate forecasting for a SaaS company is paramount. The majority of costs are tied to the headcount of employees—people cost. An accurate forecast allows the CEO to determine hiring allocations for the quarter. If they hire too many people and the quarterly bookings come in short of the company plan, costs will overrun, increasing their burn rate.

And Forego was burning money.

On the other hand, if the CEO held back on hiring due to a low forecast, but they finished the quarter far ahead, the company would fall behind in the headcount needed to support customers, enhance the product, and hire additional reps to scale the business.

Raj found himself in a very familiar place.

Stuck in a catch-22.

As I queued up the next question in my mind, I already had a feeling what his response would be.

“Sounds great, Raj. I’m excited to get started with your sales force. Who do you think it’s best for me to meet with first?”

“My managers,” he said instantly. “At least a few of them. I’d recommend you start with Jim and Andy. Jim has been a manager for more than a year, and we just promoted Andy from sales rep to manager.”

“I remember them from the QBR.”

Raj paused for a second. “Andy is frustrated. After his team missed their forecast, he told me it was very disappointing to work so hard every quarter with so little to show for it. He’s not the only one who’s frustrated.”

“Is that what prompted this call?”

“Yes, the frustration level of my managers is high. I’m worried about attrition if we don’t address these issues. I recognize that we need to change. I hope you can help us. After you speak with Andy and Jim, let’s add a few reps to gain their perspective. Once you work with them and we prove it works, we can take this to a larger audience with more managers and reps.”

With a grin, I ended the call.

This is going to be interesting.

PART II
THE MANAGERS

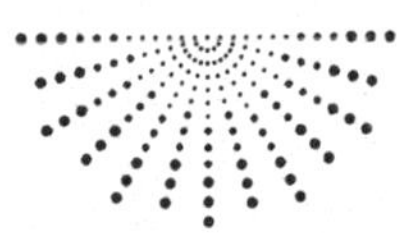

9
FIRST LINE MANAGERS

If I really wanted to help Andy and Jim, I'd eventually need to know more about them, how they managed and how their reps operated.

A week after speaking with Raj, I flew around to visit a couple of sales reps from Forego—Hannlin and Shannon. I went with them on sales calls, got a feel for their lack of process and their difficulty in understanding on which core selling issue to focus their energy. They sold as if selling were strictly an art form, no element of science or structure. No formula, procedure or means to their selling.

The following week, I took the 6:19 a.m. Amtrak to New York Penn. After a crappy Acela Café breakfast of a stale, microwaved egg sandwich, wrapped in a piece of plastic, and a tasteless, scalding cup of coffee, I turned my mind to the challenge ahead.

The seaside towns of Connecticut rolled by as I wondered what type of managers Forego would reveal. Forego was a typical startup-SaaS company that spent little-to-no money on training sales reps and zero on training their sales leaders.

CEOs have constantly told me, "Training is too expensive." CROs often said, "We don't have the time" or "We can't afford to take them away from selling."

Could they afford *not* to?

In Forego's case, definitely not.

What could possibly be more important to invest in than their sales force? Leaving the knowledge and skills of a sales force to chance was like coaching a sports team, that lacked a playbook and didn't bother with practice drills.

How did they expect to win?

That day, I felt certain Forego managers were never trained on the importance of sales fundamentals . . . at least not from a *sales leader's* perspective.

Without sales leadership training, the Forego managers would be lacking the knowledge:

- To recruit grade A players
- To assess each reps' strengths and weaknesses
- To train the reps on *what to do*. The knowledge of each step of the sales process
- To coach the reps on *how to do it*. The skills to execute steps in the sales process
- To utilize a methodology to quickly analyze deal advancement and account scenarios
- To forecast accurately
- To understand the difference between managing and leading

The forecast session during the QBR made it evident that managers at Forego used the power of their positions to drive more activity. It was a one-way transaction. The managers pushed more activities, such as email, cold calls, demos, and failed proof of concepts, in the hope that more was better. They believed more activity automatically translated to more sales.

And the reps gave them what they measured.

In reality, Forego's sales managers weren't even managing. They were simply harassing reps to do more activities.

Confusing activity with accomplishment.

Instead of tracking meaningful *indicators of deal advancement* and tangible sales process results, they *only* kept track of activity KPIs such as:

- Number of calls
- Number of emails sent
- Number of video introductions
- Number of POCs

Activity metrics without an association to indicators of deal advancement are hollow KPIs and are useless in accurately forecasting outcomes. Forego's managers were glorified scorekeepers. And glorified scorekeepers make horrible forecasters. For a sales leader, forecast accuracy is a preeminent indicator of how intimately they understand their people and the accounts on the forecast. Forego's managers were far removed from rep and account intimacy.

As usual, the Amtrak train arrived late. I hustled up the hot, smelly subway staircase and into the bustle of Penn Station. And then, up and out of the Penn Station hustle. The stale city air at

33rd Street and 7th Avenue put me face-to-face with the organized chaos of the city.

I metaphorically readied myself. Time to see if I could have a positive effect on Forego. This meeting would reveal the issues that Andy and Jim saw as first-line managers. It would set the stage for what I might teach all the first line mangers and may determine the success of the sales force—possibly the success of Forego.

After I arrived at Forego's building, someone escorted me to a conference room. I grabbed a coffee just as Jim and Andy walked in. They moved together, but out of arms' reach, and neither seemed overly friendly to the other. I extended a hand as they approached.

"Great to see both of you again," I said. "Raj has asked me to get to know you and learn about the issues your sales force faces." I grinned. "I'd like to see if I might be able help you."

10

ANDY

"Forego just promoted me from rep to manager," Andy said.

We'd settled at a long, wooden conference table—they sat across from me. The whir of the air conditioning hummed in the background, and the constant flickering from the fluorescent lighting made my eyes strain.

Andy fiddled with his coffee cup and leaned back in his chair. "And it's been . . ."

He let that thought trail off.

Andy was thirty-six years old. He stood at an athletic six-feet-three-inches tall. He'd grown up with five other brothers and no sisters in a three-bedroom, two-bathroom apartment in the tough Southie section of Boston. (Before Southie gentrified. Back when Whitey Bulger, the famous gangster who ran the Irish Mob and ruled the same streets was later indicted for nineteen murders.)

Andy's mother couldn't control the boys because his father was away from home most days and nights as an undercover FBI agent. That left his five older brothers to gang-rule the household.

Andy played baseball at Providence College, summers in the prestigious Cape Cod League, and was drafted by the St. Louis Cardinals.

His career ended early, after an unsuccessful rotator cuff surgery.

"It sucked," he said. Regret, hidden in rage, lingered in his intense gaze. "But whatever. I got over it."

He coped with his tough upbringing, absentee dad, and pro-baseball player loss by denying his pain. He remembered the things he wanted to forget. Like his brother and father taught him while growing up: Stop complaining. No one gives a shit. Screw those emotions into a jar, stuff them deep down.

Learn to live with it.

And Andy lived with it.

It was as if he had a tiny glass shard stuck in the bottom of his big toe. It was festering, but he kept his foot in the shoe and walked around, ignoring the pain, denying its existence. That had turned him into a fighter.

Anyone who'd pick a fight with Andy had better dig two graves.

His pain had generated an attitude of accepting that the world was against him. If something needed to be done, he figured he'd have to do it on his own—through brute force.

Brute force was exactly how he approached selling and sales management.

Ignore the pain. Refuse to understand there could possibly be a better way. Brute force. Just do it. Get it done. No complaining.

"I know I'm a tough manager." He half shrugged when I asked him about it. "I'd stop if I could, but how do you even do that? This is who I am. It's the only way I know how to manage."

His tough and stubborn personality held him back from both a way out of Southie and the success for which he was desperate.

11
JIM

"I've been a sales manager at Forego for a little over a year," Jim said when I turned my attention to him. "I like it. I want more."

Jim grew up in Wisconsin in a family of nine kids: five brothers, three sisters, and Jim, the baby. Being the baby with five older brothers meant Jim was constantly roughed up playing pond hockey with the big boys. Learning from his brothers made him the most talented hockey player in the family.

After playing hockey in the junior leagues, he was recruited by the University of Wisconsin Badgers, a perennial Division-I hockey powerhouse. His senior year, he earned the title of captain.

Jim had a good sense of humor, high intelligence, and a totally competitive nature in every aspect of his life. Through our basic interactions, I immediately saw that he was open to coaching.

Being part of a team was an attitude ingrained into him through hockey. A game about the name on the front of the jersey, not the name on the back. A game where teamwork is paramount. Each player's shift averages forty-five seconds, so every team member is depended upon in order to play fluidly, to do their job, to win.

No passengers. No one rides for free. Sacrifice yourself for the team every shift.

Selfless, not selfish.

As captain, Jim learned valuable lessons in leadership. Life as a Division-I captain was a job. Living with the same teammates in the dorm, for air and bus travel, and during hotel stays, and having daily practices, plus multiple games per week, allowed him to understand how each teammate was different. Not just their on-ice knowledge and skills, but, more importantly, their personal desires, goals, motivations, insecurities, and fears. He became the team sounding board.

Jim's locker-room experiences paid off as a sales leader.

He knew when and how to speak to an individual or the team as a whole. He understood the importance of acknowledging a teammate's bad day and using his empathetic ability to motivate. He understood how to get between two arguing teammates and settle a dispute, while making them see the greater common bonds they shared.

Team. Selfless.

What Jim lacked was the ability to make his team members better. Sure, he knew how to motivate them, fire them up with locker-room language, but he hadn't learned a technique to assess their knowledge levels nor the proficiency of their skills in a sales situation. He didn't understand how to evaluate why one rep was more effective in certain scenarios than another.

He possessed the desire to be a good coach but didn't know where to start. Lacking the ability to qualify where his reps were in a sales scenario left him without a constructive way to coach them. As a result, he felt constrained, uneasy.

And his team could feel it too.

12

THE OTHER FIRST LINE MANAGERS

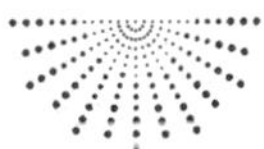

Andy represented a typical first-time, first-line sales manager at Forego. Most managers were married, lived the suburbs in a prototypical three-bedroom, two-bathroom house with a two-car garage, paid a monthly mortgage, managed a mounting number of bills, and wanted to save money for their kids' college educations. The bulk of managers were in their early to mid-thirties, staring down the sights of forty years old.

That alone increased their urgency to master selling and leadership skills *now*.

But I wanted to dig a bit deeper.

"What are the average sales managers like at Forego?" I asked.

"Super busy," Andy replied. "Always pressed for time. All managers are constantly stretched, trying to balance time between work, spouse, kids, sports, and friends. Most get up early to workout. Sometimes we stop for a drink after work to blow off steam."

"They're proven sales reps," Jim was quick to interject. "Most managers were recently promoted. They're all extremely driven people."

"Why do the reps want to get promoted?"

Jim answered "More money. More growth. More status. Some of them want to get promoted through the ranks with the ultimate goal to become CRO someday."

An interesting observation from Jim, who had admitted that he wanted more from Forego. I had a feeling that was his ambition, but I couldn't get a definite read on Andy.

"Most of the sales managers think managing means becoming a rep's friend," Andy said.

He was correct. I'd seen this before. Managers came into the position, ready to be buddies and earn friendships. But reps didn't need more friends. Most had plenty of friends and some were trying to get rid of a few.

What they needed was someone to teach, coach, motivate, and lead them. Someone to help them develop their sales craft, make more money, and win.

Reps needed someone they could respect.

"Many of the recently promoted managers haven't fully realized that the sales leadership role isn't about them," Jim said. "They think they're a super sales rep and have to sell all the deals for their reps. They don't really see that the combined successes of their reps are what determines their success as a manager."

Check the manager comp plan, I thought.

In other words, the sales managers were still selfish. They hadn't realized that the success of their reps came from how well *they* trained, developed, and coached the reps. The newer managers believed their reps all had the same strengths, weaknesses, desires, and motivations as they did, so they managed them as if they were all the same.

Cookie cutter.

They weren't educating their reps on how to prospect, build a pipeline of qualified deals, understand and use the sales process, prepare themselves for their next meeting, or analyze their sales calls.

"Since our management style is focused solely on performing activities," Jim said, "our reps learn almost nothing from their managers. They're like gerbils on a wheel. Every day, every week, every month, performing the same activities, managed by the same KPIs. Never learning anything new."

"How unfulfilling is that?"

"Very unfulfilling, because many reps are leaving the sales force," Andy said.

"They're leaving because they're not learning and not making money.", added Jim.

"What about the more tenured managers?" I asked after a sip of bitter coffee. "Are they managing differently?"

"The more experienced managers understand by now that their reps are different," Jim said. "But, like most of us, they have a difficult time assessing which rep is better and why. That makes it hard to know how to coach and train our reps."

Andy nodded.

Those same managers were awakening to the realization they were consciously incompetent. Relying on sheer activity was no longer working. More busyness didn't convert to more closed sales. They knew what they were doing was wrong, but they didn't know what to change, let alone how.

Cognitive dissonance.

Unfortunately, old habits die hard.

13
WHERE THE QBR WENT WRONG

A quick break gave me a chance to stand up, move around, and think through Jim and Andy's relationship within the company. While I poured another cup of coffee, my thoughts unfolded.

Although eager to learn, Andy was nothing but a teeming ball of impatience. His business relationship with Jim had grown obviously tense and cumbersome. No doubt, in Andy's mind, Jim was a competitor to beat, not a teammate to learn from. Andy's natural instinct was to withdraw when losing. Just like he'd learned growing up in Southie.

Withdraw, poker face, pick your fight, attack.

The world is against you.

Jim, on the other hand, clearly knew what he didn't know, but he wasn't sure what step to take next. How could he set an example and successfully lead his team? He seemed as frustrated as Andy, but neither was in control of their teams and their accounts.

The growth of Forego from a startup that sold features and functions into accounts to a company that sold a more complex product platform was common. So were Andy's and Jim's personal transitions from reps to managers. The challenges of moving from an individual contributor to managing people with different personalities and skillsets was a difficult hurdle.

But not a new one.

When I returned to the table, they were already there. "So," I said. "Let's switch topics a little bit. First, how did your teams finish last quarter?"

"Just below quota for mine," Jim said with a slight grimace.

"Eighty percent of our quota," Andy muttered.

"How did that make you feel?"

"Lousy," Jim immediately replied. "Like a loser. I hate not beating my quota."

Andy's hands had balled into fists, and a tic appeared in his jaw. "Frustrating. We work *so* hard. Day in. Day out. It's disappointing to finish below a goal every quarter."

"It's not just us, either," Jim said. "My team experiences the same frustration. How much longer can they continue to run hard and never have line of sight to the money they expected to make?"

"For those reasons, we're losing reps." Andy glanced at Jim for a moment. "Our sales rep attrition is at thirty-five percent, and I predict it's growing."

Dreadful.

Even though many SaaS startups have a twenty to twenty-five percent attrition rate, thirty-five percent and growing is problematic. It's a major problem to scale when the attrition rate exceeds the new hire rate.

In addition to not training and coaching their reps, these managers were most likely poor recruiters. My gut said they were poor at everything, but I wanted to get the subject back to the QBR. Find out what they really understood.

"What are the main reasons for having a forecast session at a QBR?"

Both of them paused for a second, and I let the silence ride.

Jim finally broke it when he said, "Well . . . I guess we should use it to understand our selling issues. For example, to figure out how effective our reps are at selling. Or to better understand our competitions' strategies in our potential accounts? Or to identify the product and support issues we have."

Andy chimed in with a completely surprising response. "We should compare different reps. Particularly their individual selling capabilities. We should view the change in every reps' quarter-to-quarter development."

So why didn't they?

It comes down to knowing *how* to do that.

When reps walk through their deals, managers should ask proper inspection questions that probe deeper. Root questions that involve second-, third-, and fourth-level analyses. Questions that drive to the heart of selling issues in each account to understand why a deal is, or is not, progressing through the sales process. And provide coaching on the next logical step in the process.

GAMING THE CRM SYSTEM

"Do you require the reps to enter their deals into a CRM system?" I asked while I scribbled a few notes down.

"Prior to the QBR," Jim said, "the reps must put their forecasted deals into the CRM system and update the forecast every Friday. From there, we obtain a view of the forecast from each rep and a total rollup of our team."

At least they had that, but a CRM system didn't qualify reps or deals. It was incapable of analyzing the selling situation in an account. It was simply a dumb repository of information.

"Reps only put information into the CRM system and update it weekly because management requires it," Jim said. "Not because it's a useful tool, and it certainly doesn't increase their productivity. We get it. We were once reps."

"But that's only one of the problems." Andy leaned forward a little, and it seemed like some of the tightness had faded from his shoulders. "The reps are asked to update the CRM weekly on Friday, so the data are never real time. If we view the forecast on Wednesday, most of the information we're using is from the prior Friday."

CRM systems posed other problems as well. Reps were free to place a deal in the CRM system at any stage of the process. That meant they could intentionally place deals into later stages of the sales process to inflate their forecasts.

Or, more commonly, due to poor qualification skills, they unintentionally placed deals into later stages of the forecast due to "happy ears," a term that refers to a rep hearing only what they want to hear from a customer and letting themselves believe a deal is more qualified than it really is.

"And even our best reps' game the CRM system with their largest and most highly qualified deals," Jim said. "They intentionally place deals into early stages of the sales process, so management at all levels doesn't call them weekly for deal updates."

Andy added, "We know there's usually a discrepancy between the stage of the deal in the CRM system and reality. That's why we have to have forecast sessions."

At this point, I leaned back in my chair and asked a favorite question. "As managers, what do you think you lack in becoming better forecasters?"

"Consistency," Jim said immediately. "Each manager analyzes deals differently because we use different versions of the sales process."

Without admitting to his own personal brute force method, Andy explained, "In addition to everyone using a different sales process, we don't have a constructive method to analyze every deal, so managers hammer reps with questions in the hope that it will reveal an accurate assessment of the account situation."

Interesting admittance from Andy.

"So, let's roll this back a little bit," I said. "What are the negative consequences for you as managers when there isn't a common method to analyze account situations?"

"Take the Thompson deal from Kathleen as an example," Andy said. "Deals hang around the forecast for several quarters until they finally die. We need a way to know the deal isn't going to close so we work only on deals that will close.

"Not to mention how frustrating and stressful it is when deals fall out of the forecast one or two weeks before the end of the quarter," he added. "I'm always uncomfortable and totally stressed at the end of the quarter. I never feel like we're in control of deals, so the last two weeks of every quarter becomes a frantic nightmare as we try to make the forecast.

"Time management sucks as well. I spend too much time with my reps calling on unqualified accounts, that either never close or take too long to close, for small deal sizes."

Andy shook his head.

Their issues were far greater than they'd expressed. I didn't feel like they were ready to "throw in the towel." They were certainly committed, smart, and driven to succeed. I could work with them.

With a deep breath, I said, "Thank you for being completely transparent during our discussion today. It was very informative. I understand many of the issues you and your teams face, and it was good to get to learn more about you personally. Tomorrow morning, we'll meet with the rest of the first-line managers and see if we can find a way out of this."

14
MANAGER PRIORITIES

When I was first promoted to manage a team of sales reps from Santa Barbara to San Diego, I had no idea what I was supposed to do.

I knew three things at the time:

1. My compensation plan told me that I maximize my earnings by helping my sales reps sell. The more they sold, the more I'd get paid. Simple.
2. As a new manager, I didn't understand what was important internally.
3. That I didn't want to be like the other managers, who were always in their cubicles. How could they be so busy in a cubicle when their comp plan was the same as mine?

When I arrived on my first day, I chose the cubicle left vacant by the previous underperforming sales manager, who had left the company.

At that time, laptops were a thing but not the Internet. The vast amount of paper in my cubicle quickly overwhelmed me. Loose-leaf binders filled three bookshelves, and paper files stuffed three large file cabinets. More paper overflowed from the inbox on my desk.

Frustrated, I went downstairs to see John, who was the head of the Shipping and Receiving Department. He and some other friends, who I played softball with during weeknights, worked down there.

"Hey, John," I said. "Grab a few guys, some hand trucks, and empty boxes, and follow me upstairs to my office."

So, he did.

We stood at my cubicle for a few minutes. Then I said, "Can you help me box all the files and every item in the bookshelves and then throw them into the dumpster outside?"

Disbelieving, John looked at me and said, "What? You want us to throw everything in the dumpster?"

"Yes."

"Uh . . . OK. Boys, let's get it done."

Within minutes, John and his team had cleared my bookshelves and file cabinets. Felt great.

After tidying everything up, I positioned the mail inbox on the far-left side of my desk and placed the trashcan just below it. Every day, I went on sales calls with my team. At night, when we returned to the office, I would take all the papers in my inbox and throw them into the trash bin.

After a few weeks, a couple of people would ask if they could speak with me.

"I sent you paperwork with a request several times, but I haven't heard back."

So, I'd ask them a few questions:

Why is it important?
Is it urgent?
Who says that it is important?
Why do I need to do it now?
Will it help my sales team sell more?

The majority of the time, it wasn't that important, nor was it urgent, and it wouldn't help my team. It was driven by a low level person trying to look busy.

Through this process, I discovered what was truly important. And that most things were unimportant because many people ask you to do things for *their* reasons. They wanted to *look busy*. "Take this survey," "respond to this email," "read this report," "please show up for this meeting." It all told their boss they were doing something meaningful.

Bureaucrats.

So many sales leaders in my company at the time took the bait. They let other people's priorities become their priorities. Most of the compensation plans for sales leaders are simple and very clear:

Your reps sell; you get paid.

Compensation plans are meant to drive a certain behavior. The comp plan should drive sales managers to do what is fundamentally necessary to help their people maximize sales.

I quickly realized that I was paid to recruit, train, and develop my people to maximize sales and so they could eventually take my place when I get promoted.

Responding to a multitude of meaningless phone conversations, bureaucratic conference calls, and internal meetings with no specific prerequisites, written agenda, or defined outcomes wasted my time.

So, I stopped.

When I focused on recruiting grade A players, developing their knowledge and skills during sales calls, and leading them, we all became better at selling *as a team*. When I taught my team to master the fundamentals of the game, they performed better. They learned new competencies. We sold more. They made more money. We all grew and made more money.

Forego needed to focus on what was important.

The fundamentals.

The basics.

15
EXPLAINING THE BASICS

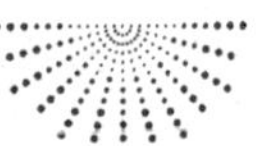

That night, after meeting with Jim and Andy, I stayed at the Citizen M hotel at 50th and Broadway, one of the newer, boutique, (read: minimalist) hotels in the city. The day had been informative, and I felt ready for tomorrow.

After a run in Central Park the next morning, I showered, grabbed a Starbucks, and took the elevator to the meeting room with all the first-line managers.

This time, I could feel something in the air when I walked inside and spoke briefly with a few of them. Anticipation. Uncertainty. Whatever it was, a sea full of eyes looked at me. Andy and Jim were amongst them—sitting apart from each other.

After reintroducing myself to the group, I explained that I was here to positively change their life as sales managers.

"Raj asked me to help advise you on leading and managing your teams, defining a sales process, qualifying deals and forecasting accurately. Before you can lead a team to become proficient with the basic knowledge of how to play the game—or coach someone on the basic skills to play the game—you need to simplify things into the basics of the game.

"A good friend of mine, Cedric, told me a story that emphasizes why the basics are so important to master in any game. So, I'm going to start with a tale."

THE FOX AND THE HEDGEHOG

There is a fox named Sly Smartass.

Sly is a very capable creature with a host of enviable assets. He has always been a sure winner. Sleek, cunning, and agile, he also has great eyesight and can run almost forty miles per hour.

On the other hand, there is a hedgehog named Billy Basics.

Billy Basics was born a genetic mix-up between a porcupine and an armadillo. This left Billy with poor eyesight, so he has to rely on hearing and his keen sense of smell to get around.

He's so slow that he can't even run.

Billy Basics waddles.

Sly Smartass is nocturnal and likes to hunt when the sun goes down. He waits in silence and stays out of sight because he loves subtlety over brute force. Sly crouches down to camouflage himself, then leaps out and lands on top of his prey with a scream. "Aha, I've got you now!"

Billy Basics is also nocturnal. He hides in vacated burrows, under rocks, or in thick vegetation. When Billy Basics thinks he is being attacked, he rolls into a tight ball in self-defense, causing all of his 5,000 spines to point out. Then he lets out a loud snort, like a large hog.

When Sly tries to attack Billy Basics, Billy's acute smell and hearing alerts him to the attack. Into a ball of spikes, he goes. When Sly sees Billy's impenetrable defence, he calls off his attack.

Every day, the same battle occurs.

With the same outcome.

Sly, armed with cunning, agile assets, creates a new change in his strategy to attack Billy Basics. But Billy, sensing a new attack, relies on the basics. He uses his guiding principles—his fundamentals, which are now natural instincts—to fend off Sly Smartass's multiple-angle attacks.

Sly Smartass sees the world in all of its complexity. He pursues many methods to attack Billy at the same time. He always believes there must be a new strategy or a new way. He constantly changes his methods and never integrates his thinking into a few guiding principles.

Some say that Billy Basics is stupid. On deeper reflection, he's quite clever. He understands that the essence of profound insight is simplicity.

Billy simplifies his world into a few basic principles that guide his everyday plans. No matter how complex the world becomes, Billy Basics reduces all challenges and dilemmas into a few simple hedgehog principles.

He has mastered the fundamentals. The basics.

Simplicity becomes a limitless gift presented to individuals that master the fundamentals.

At this point, the sales leaders murmured to each other, clearly catching on to the main point of the story.

Each of them had their own sales process and own way to analyze deals, none of which ever seemed to work on a consistent basis. It seemed to me that they were ready to start simplifying their lives by learning the basics and mastering the fundamentals, which was right where I wanted them.

Billy Basics would become an imaginary hero at Forego.

The best place to start was with the basic items that the management team, as a whole, lacked during the QBR. Those foundational items would make them constructive qualifiers, potent forecasters and more effective leaders, immediately.

16
THE BASICS

BASIC #1: A COMMON VOCABULARY

First thing on the agenda was a common vocabulary.

I'm constantly surprised to learn that sales teams don't have a common vocabulary. The leader asks questions, the rep answers, but they aren't really communicating. They *believe* they're communicating, but they're not understanding each other, because they use different definitions for the same words.

"Your forecasting session revealed a lack of common vocabulary," I said to them. "There was an obvious disparity between what the reps said and what the managers asked. I was curious, so during a few coffee breaks at your QBR, I picked some commonly used terms and asked different reps and managers to explain their definitions.

"For instance, when I asked, 'What is a Champion?' I received four different definitions. Who is the 'Economic Buyer?' Different answers. 'What's the difference between a Champion and a coach?' 'What is a technical buyer?' Every answer came back different."

A few of the sales managers fidgeted. My eyes skated over to Andy, who frowned at the floor in front of him. Even Jim seemed thoughtful. I could imagine them running their own terms through their minds.

"The team must adopt a common vocabulary for all your sales terminology. It's fundamental to effective communication and it's the basis for accurate qualification and rep development.", I added.

Perhaps now they could see that it was impossible to operate a sales force, describe an account scenario, qualify a deal, or run a forecast session when different people had different definitions of the same words.

BASIC #2: LISTENING

"Did you know that people can listen and comprehend 250 words per minute?" I asked.

A few heads shook, and low mumbles followed.

"But most people speak at only 150 words per minute. What does that create? *Impatience.*

Since we hear and comprehend faster than most people speak, our minds wander. We get impatient.

"You were guilty of impatience. Do you know how I know?" I asked. "I observed you at the QBR. Your questions and your advice were ineffective. The reps were trying to tell you about the account situation, but you were too impatient to listen to what they said. You interrupted them and you told them what *you thought* was happening in the account. You told them they could do better."

There's no benefit in simply telling someone to perform better when they're struggling. You're yelling "SELL" to a struggling sales rep. It's like yelling "SWIM" to a drowning man.

We often get ahead of ourselves in conversations, especially when, as leaders, we hold the power. Sales managers in a QBR tend to think about their next question, think about what they are going to say, instead of really *listening* to the reps.

Of course, they may have heard what the rep said, but do they truly comprehend?

Likely not.

More efficient questions are formed when the manager seeks to understand, not to be right.

"Raise your hand," I said, "if you believe you listened carefully, took the time to digest the reps' information, and countered with a pertinent question or constructive coaching feedback."

No hands lifted into the air. I grinned to lighten the sudden tension that had filled the room.

With a smile, I said, "We all have a mouth that closes and ears that don't; that should remind all of us to listen carefully. Try to listen with the intent to understand—not the intent to reply.

"When you really listen and try to deeply understand, you ask better probing questions. What was the rep leaving out of their description? What did they really mean by that last statement? What is actually happening in the account?"

Ineffective listening generates ineffective questions

BASIC #3: BE HERE

I turned to a whiteboard behind me and wrote down the third basic they needed: Be HERE.

To be a great listener, you have to be *HERE*. Present. Turn off all the other distractions and be in the moment. Multiple social media channels, emails, texts, calls, and alerts are all vying for your attention and distracting you from being in the moment.

Most people are in *a constant state of partial attention*. Silence the phone, close the laptop, forget about what just happened, what you did last weekend, what you're going to say next, or what you're going to do later. Be HERE. Force yourself into a deep listening experience.

Managers must immerse themselves in the story the rep tells.

Live in the story.

Be in the account.

Picture the rep at the account.

- Where are they in the sales process?
- Were they speaking with a coach, a Champion, or the enemy?
- What level of the account were they speaking?
- What were they trying to achieve?
- What did they do to succeed?
- What caused them to fail?
- What were the surrounding circumstances?
- What were the account dynamics?

I studied the faces in the room and decided a little tougher honesty wouldn't hurt them.

"Your heads were somewhere other than in the moment, in the room with the reps. I think you were too worried and anxious about your own forecasts. You were only concerned with how the reps' numbers would affect you. Anxious to get to the final number so you could see how the total forecast result would affect you for the quarter.

"Am I wrong?"

No one countered.

"You weren't in the moment," I concluded. "You weren't *here*. You have to be *here* to be a good listener. You have to be an effective listener to be a constructive sales leader. Your reps deserve that from you."

BASIC #4: INTUITION

What the Sales Management team at Forego didn't realize yet was that all these issues grew off each other. Compounded. After I wrote the next one on the whiteboard—Intuition—a surprised look that said, "tell me more" overtook each person's face. A look that also told me they never expected intuition to be one of the basics.

"Maybe you don't trust your intuition," I said. "Maybe you've never experimented with the ability of using your intuition to help you analyze and make decisions. Maybe you haven't utilized your intuition often enough to trust it. Perhaps you believe everything needs to be addressed and answered only by the analysis of facts.

"Well? Let's try to put an end to it."

At this point, every eyebrow in the room rose.

To be an effective sales leader, you need to use your intuition to help you perceive the situation. Most people only analyze situations and make decisions with their head. They never rely on their second powerful decision engine: their gut.

A sixth sense, street smarts, intuition.

Intuition is an effective ally when used to qualify opportunities coach reps and sell. It helps any salesperson or leader sense the exact status of the situation. Intuition helps us "feel" a situation. If effectively utilized, it's a secondary information processing unit.

It's amazing that we often need permission to allow ourselves to tap into this superpower.

"When combined with the situational facts your brain processes," I continued, "your intuition allows you to ask more perceptive questions. Triangulate between the rep, your mind and your gut. *Triangulate to the right conclusion.*"

A hand rose at the back. "How does that work exactly?" an uncertain voice asked.

"You have to train yourself on the other basics," I quickly replied. "To utilize intuition, first, you have to trust it. Then, you need to be *here, present in the moment.* You can't feel and intuit if you're not *here* and keenly listening to your rep with a clear mind. Listen to understand, listen to feel, listen to sense. Don't listen to talk."

In another word, extreme *focus.*

"Your intuition needs a clear, open mind. It won't work if it's competing with other distracting thoughts, fears, or prejudices of your own past experiences."

When no further questions came, I turned back to the board.

BASIC #5 SELF AWARENESS

I wrote the next basic skill on the white board: Self-awareness. And I recommended that each of the managers take some time to reflect and understand how their own character traits effected the people on their team.

Self-awareness is critical to selling and paramount to being a leader.

Take an assessment of yourself:

- What are your positive characteristics, and what role do they play motivating your people?
- Which of your negative character traits may have a detrimental effect on the willingness of your people to engage you in discussion and utilize your coaching during sales calls and forecast reviews?

Without intimate self-awareness, you may not understand a negative character trait that prevents you from maximizing your effectiveness as a leader.

BASIC #6: TRANSFORMATIONAL MINDSET

"As managers, you hammered the reps with questions during the forecast review because you could. Your position as a leader provides an inherent *power over the reps*. You're in charge. But having the power of position doesn't make this a one-way street. When the forecasting session becomes a one-way interrogation, the reps will tell you what they think you want to hear. Is that a good thing?"

A chorus of *no's* rippled through the room.

"Right. When you only use the power of your position, your interaction and relationship with your reps becomes transactional. Reps give you what you want in return for not being punished. They don't need penalties. They don't need interrogations or simple transactions with you. They need coaching. They want to learn. They want to be developed."

"You want your reps to be comfortable giving bad news, early. I have a saying that, 'Bad news can't wait'." As a leader, I want my reps to be able to share bad news quickly, so we have enough time to remedy the situation. If your reps are in a transaction-oriented relationship with you, they aren't going to feel comfortable sharing bad news for fear of penalty."

"If the reps knew what to do, they wouldn't need you."

I leaned my hands on the table and met several of their gazes.

"Time to step up. Time to be a leader, a coach, not someone who only penalizes. Being a true leader is the opposite. A leader's relationship with their people should be transformational, not transactional."

They want to be transformed.

The leader needs to have an *intimate* understanding of how their people work.

They need to view every rep as an individual with different motivations, desires, strengths, weaknesses, and fears. A leader aligns motivations and desires and shows the rep why it's in their best interest to do what needs to be done. The reps know that if they can achieve the leader's vision, it will in turn transform their abilities, their knowledge, their careers and lives.

That is a transformational mindset.

It all starts with understanding why they joined your company. What they hoped to achieve when they made the decision to work for you. Sit down with them and document their annual goals, financial goals and career goals.

From what I knew of Jim, he was already grounded as a leader. He saw the team members separately and knew they wanted to achieve different things. He could bring them together as a team, but he didn't know how to transform them as individuals, how to guide them to be better sales reps individually. Develop them to win more.

He nodded his head as I spoke, clearly aligned with what I said. But Andy stared at the floor, brow heavy.

I kept going.

"It's your job to coach your reps based on careful analysis of account scenarios and their skillsets. The interaction needs to be an equal exchange: coaching advice for account information. They should be comfortable when they give you their honest assessment of the account, not feel like they'll be penalized. In return, you assist them, help them develop and win for their own advancement and the betterment of the team."

I paused and said, "Transformational."

Jim asked, "We've heard you loud and clear on transformation of our people. What I also hear you saying is that as leaders, *transformation needs to be our purpose*."

"Yes, that's right Jim. When people are being transformed, you'll see your attrition numbers decrease and your promotion and quota attainment numbers increase. More importantly, people will respond to your coaching, their transformation and there will be a more positive interaction between you and your people." I responded.

"If that's our purpose, how will we know when we've totally transformed our people?" Jim questioned.

"When they are self-sufficient. When they no longer need you, your job is done. When you know that they can take your place as the team leader, your job is complete. When that occurs, it's a win-win. Not only do your reps win, but you win because you've maximized the productivity and performance of your team," I answered.

BASIC #7 DON'T BE A GLORIFIED SCOREKEEPER

Andy wondered, "That makes sense but where do we start?"

"Today, you're managing your people only through activity with no focus on accomplishment. You inspect activity-based KPIs with *no analysis* of why they achieve or don't achieve the KPIs. And, certainly, without any indication of how effective those KPIs are in leading to closing deals."

In short, they were sleepwalking on the job.

Mindlessly doing the same things over and over without differing results.

"You're *glorified scorekeepers*," I told them. "You aren't understanding the why. Why deals advance or don't advance in the sales process. Why a rep is successful or struggling."

You're not inspiring your people or developing your reps so they can succeed. How long do you think people can work for you when all you do is inspect activity only but not inspire, coach and develop?

"How inspiring is it to work for a scorekeeper?" I asked.

"It can't be too inspiring if you have a thirty-five percent rep attrition rate. There's a saying that, 'People don't leave companies, they leave managers.'"

I think that hurt.

So, where do you start?

First, you start with *inspiration.*

When you become intimate with your people's strengths and weaknesses, goals, aspirations, frustrations, insecurities and fears, you know what drives and inspires them.

Second, by knowing the strength of their knowledge and skills to effectively execute the sales process, you'll need to constantly *coach and develop* them for success.

Third, only after you've inspired and coached have you earned the right to *inspect* them.

It's not a one-time thing. It's a never-ending, personally tailored loop:

Inspire
Coach and Develop
Inspect

When it's time to inspect, you want to inspect the WHY. Why deals progress and why deals stall. Analyze the WHY. Help your people understand the WHY. Then coach them on what they need to change, what they need to know and what their next logical step should be.

BASIC #8 INTENTIONAL OUTCOMES

Andy asked, "Are you saying we should intentionally think inspire, coach, and inspect?"

I answered, "For sure. We discussed why your interaction with your people can't be transactional. It needs to be a win-win. Start with an objective for every meeting. If your intention is a win-win for you and your team, then, before any meeting with your reps, ask yourself, 'What is my desired outcome for the rep and the team?'"

As a leader, *you can't just show up for a meeting without intention.*

You need to understand what you expect from your people, and they need to understand what to expect from you. You need to understand how you will add tangible value and how to drive toward a desired outcome for you and the rep. Without striving toward a desired outcome, you are not intentionally helping your people to transform.

BASIC #9 KEEP IT SIMPLE

You are a sales leader. Don't over complicate things that aren't complex. You job is to take complex things and make them easy to understand for both your reps and your customers. Too many sales leaders overcomplicate presentations and communications with needless wording. Communicate clearly and in simple terms for people to understand. If your grandmother won't understand it, it's too complex.

BASIC #10: URGENT CURIOSITY

The first dry-erase marker I used was dry, so I threw it in the trash can where it belonged. Why did people put dried-up markers back on the whiteboard tray?

The next marker squeaked as I finished writing. I capped it and tossed it back into the tray. The captive audience stared hard at me now, several of them still scribbling notes.

"And finally, you lacked genuine curiosity," I said.

Andy's head snapped up at this, so I pointed to him. "Do you think you were truly curious, Andy?"

"Yes."

"Were you listening intently to understand?" I questioned.

"Kind of."

"Really? Did you ask good qualifying questions?" I asked.

He straightened confidently. "Yes."

"Were they good examining questions based on the reps account scenario? Or were they the same common questions for each rep? Were they cookie-cutter? Were they superficial?"

A long breath blew out of him. Resigned, he shook his head. "No. They weren't good, probing questions."

"I agree." I grinned. "Your questions didn't originate from a point of genuine curiosity and a longing to understand *why*. Why the reps are struggling in their accounts. What do you need to do to help them change the situation?"

"You know and I know that good questions arise out of a genuine interest, a genuine curiosity to understand."

THE GREATEST SALESMAN

This was a perfect segue for me to tell a story about the greatest salesperson I'd ever met.

Carlo Carpanelli came from Bologna, Italy.

Perennially, Carlo was the top sales rep in every company he worked for. He always sold the company's largest deals to the largest companies in the Emilia Romagna region of Italy.

Companies like GD, Marchesini, Ducati, and Ferrari.

I always wondered what made Carlo the top rep. Perhaps his incredible depth of character. He had a multitude of character traits most people could only wish to possess:

High intelligence
Keen sense of human behavior
Complete self-awareness
Powerful situational intuition
Courage
Unflappability

However, with all his assets, I always wondered if there was one trait that separated Carlo from the rest of his peers. Maybe that trait could make the rest of the sales force just as productive as Carlo.

One day, I saw that trait in person.

Carlo and I had just finished making all-day sales calls in Ferrari. Ferrari, a world-famous brand, home of the "Prancing Horse," headquartered in Maranello, Italy.

You could almost *feel* the prestige of the Ferrari brand as we walked the historic hallways that Enzo Ferrari had built. The incredible legacy of his wins at Formula 1, racing with the Scuderia Ferrari team and renowned production cars.

We made sales calls on multiple Ferrari directors throughout the day and even had the pleasure of dining with Piero Ferrari in the executive dining room for lunch. All day long, during our interactions with Ferrari leaders, I noticed Carlo's curiosity. He was curious about everything.

Curious to understand *why*.

Curious as to *why* things were the way they were.

So curious, in fact, that Carlo was never offended by someone's differing opinion, someone degrading his product or speaking down to him. For Carlo, that was an opportunity to understand *why*.

Curiosity.

After all the calls, we stepped into the crisp spring air in front of the entrance. As the sun started to set, Carlo stopped and asked me a question. "What did we learn on the calls today?"

While I summarized what we had learned, I realized there was a new set of unanswered questions. A puzzled expression came to his face. Right then, several employees drove past us through the open archway of the Ferrari building. I watched their sleek forms slip by for a second.

When I turned back to Carlo, he had walked away from me and back to the front door of Ferrari.

"Carlo, where are you going?" I yelled.

"Back into Ferrari to get the answers," he called over his shoulder. "I'm going to do it in Italian so I can get the answers quickly."

In that moment, I recognized that Carlo had been carrying me all day. My not speaking Italian had been a hindrance to his ability to perform. As I stood there, I also realized something more important: The character trait that separated Carlo from his peers wasn't his intelligence, his keen sense of human behavior, his street smarts, or his amazing intuition. I'd hired many sales reps with all of those traits.

It was curiosity that separated Carlo.

Sincere curiosity, which is never offensive.

He had an earnest need to understand and a desire to know the answers, right now.

He had an *urgency* to understand.

Why wait until tomorrow if you can know now? To leave for home without the answers to his open questions would drive Carlo absolutely bananas.

In other words, he had an *urgent curiosity.*

Most sales reps would have driven home and, in a few days, tried to schedule follow-up meetings with Ferrari stakeholders. Carlo, knowing that the people with the answers were still inside the building, obtained their responses immediately.

That's why he was different.

He knew time was his enemy.

TIME IS YOUR ENEMY

"The reason that you as a sales manager," I said, "and your reps should have urgent curiosity is because *time is your enemy.* There's never enough time for follow-up sessions with customers. In an average quarter, there are only sixty-one working days. Rep productivity is turbocharged when you and your reps have an acute curiosity to fully understand a sales situation."

Urgent curiosity.

Jim lifted a hand. "Wait, John. Why did you say there are only sixty-one days in a quarter? Quarters are ninety days."

A common issue in sales is an overestimation of the time to sell during a quarter, so I broke the math down for them on the white board. While a quarter is ninety days, not all of those are working days.

12 weeks per quarter = 24 weekend days

90 days in the quarter - 24 weekend days = 66 days to sell

66 days to sell - 3 holiday days (average) per quarter = 63 selling days per quarter

Those sixty-three days don't include time off for vacation. There's an average of ten vacation days per year, so we'll say two vacation days per quarter.

Only sixty-one selling days in a quarter.

"Sixty-one days isn't a lot of time to build qualified pipeline and move forecasted deals through the sales process," I said. "That's why urgent curiosity is critical to compressing sales cycles."

The sales managers blinked at me.

The silence made it abundantly clear that they were thinking, digesting the information.

At that point, I paused the meeting. Time to take a break and let everyone absorb the lessons they'd just learned. Afterward, Raj, Dennis, and sales reps Shannon, Carlos, Hannlin, and Kathleen were going to join us.

17

SALES PROCESS BENEFITS

When we reconvened after a break, and everyone sat down, I decided to move past a few of the leadership basics and get straight to the point of discussing the basics of the sales process from differing viewpoints.

On the whiteboard, I wrote four things down under a heading.

Who Benefits from a Sales Process:

1. Sales Reps
2. Sales Managers
3. Executive Management
4. The Customer

"Why is a sales process important to a sales rep?" I asked.

Silence reigned in the room until Andy said, "A sales process should be a map for a sales rep to follow. It should have directions and steps that a rep should perform, from start to finish, to close a deal."

"But why is that meaningful for the rep to follow?"

Before Andy could answer, Hannlin jumped into the discussion with a charming grin. "If we follow the process and don't skip steps, it should result in higher win rates, larger average deal sizes, and increased deal velocity."

"Correct. Everyone benefits massively from a well-defined sales process."

But Hannlin and other sales reps had been skipping steps in the sales process. I wasn't about to let him off the hook.

"Later we'll discuss why the team needs to slow down the early stages of the sales process to be effective in the mid- to final stages," I said, "but suffice it to say that *not* following the steps causes low proof-of-concept win rates *and* smaller-than-average deal sizes. Think those are worth following steps for?"

Hannlin nodded.

I pointed to Jim. "What does a sales process do for sales managers?"

"It gives sales leaders consistency across the sales force."

"Do you have one?"

A sheepish expression crossed his face. "Um, no. Today, every manager has their own version of the sales process."

"Great. What do you think is most lacking?"

"A common playbook with a common language to discuss accounts with our reps," he said. "With achievements necessary to successfully complete the steps within each stage."

"Tangible evidence that they completed the stage," Andy piped up.

Jim nodded to him. "Agreed. That would allow us to understand the specific details of each stage, which would highlight where reps may be underperforming. That information helps us coach them through the process."

Andy jumped back in, "Knowing which step in a stage our sales rep is facing difficulty completing gives us an understanding of a particular knowledge and/or skill gap that needs to be addressed."

"And what are the benefits to a customer?"

Shannon volunteered, "Through a well-defined sales process, the customer completely understands why the product they buy differs from other products and specifically how it solves their pains."

Jim added, "They'll understand the tangible value they get from a product."

So, I turned to Raj and Dennis, who sat close together at the edge of the room. They both straightened.

"If your entire sales force adhered to a structured sales process, what could be a potential outcome for you?" I asked.

Raj's expression illuminated. "So much!" he said. "A more efficient use of resources, for one. They'll know why they are winning and why they are losing. They'd be more effective in accounts, which also increases productivity."

"A higher win rate and larger deal sizes should generate a more accurate forecast. There would be more consistency and predictability each quarter," Dennis said.

Raj added. "And we'd gain valuable insight into the people, process, and product issues preventing the sales force from being highly productive. A win for everyone at Forego."

EXIT CRITERIA

The sales process is more than just something that's applied to reps and managers. It needs to become a functional part of operating the business. Without a well-defined sales process—and a technique to hold reps accountable to completing each stage—the reps will be less productive and, as a result, forecast incorrectly.

Each sales stage needs to have defined, tangible action steps. *And each stage should have exit criteria based on verifiable customer events.*

"Gates," I explained, "are simply the exit criteria between each stage of the sales process. Reps need to accomplish the exit criteria to *open the gate* and allow the deal to move the next step of the process.

"Gates can also have KPIs, which measure effectiveness and deal velocity. For instance, what percentage of deals from one stage transitioned to the next stage, and how long did they take to transition."

Of course, the downside of not having deals in their proper stages has a huge net negative effect on the forecast. If every rep on a team moves just one deal to the next unqualified step in the sales process, the net negative compounds as you move up in sales leadership.

I pointed to Andy. "Let's say five of your reps misrepresent one forecasted deal at $100,000. That has a $500,000 net negative effect. At a second-line manager level, with three first-line managers and fifteen reps, that's a 1.5-million-dollar misrepresentation."

My gaze moved to Raj and Dennis. "At the CRO and CEO level, where decisions are made based on the forecast, the aggregation of deals in the wrong stages compounds even further."

Raj and Dennis's emphatic nods punctuated the silence more than words ever could have.

PART III
THE B2B SALES PROCESS

18
SALES PROCESS EXAMPLE

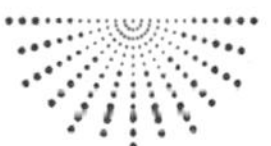

Performed correctly, the sales process should yield a positive business outcome for the rep, the manager, and the customer. A win-win-win scenario. But I still had to show them *what* a proper sales process contained.

On the whiteboard, I wrote the chronological order of a typical B2B sales process.

1. Discovery
2. Scoping
3. Economic Buyer Meeting
4. Validation Event
5. Business Case and Final Proposal
6. Negotiate and Close

"Now," I said, turning back to the room. "These six stages of a sales process are an example for us to use during our discussions. These stages are typical for most, but not all B2B enterprise SaaS sales forces. Some may need to adjust the steps we discuss within each stage, and the stages themselves may change to align with the customer's buying process.

"Let's see exactly what each stage of a sales process looks like."

DISCOVERY

"OK," I began after another sip of coffee and a few minutes for them to get their notepads and laptops ready. "Tell me a little about the discovery stage of the sales process. Andy, what do you think it is?"

"Discovery is when we learn if the client is *buying what we're selling*."

"That's really good. Discovery should qualify accounts into, or out of, your forecast. What specific information should your reps obtain during discovery, Jim?"

"Pain points, problems, or a corporate initiative."

"And *how the customer does things today*," Andy said. "Their current process, their environment and the associated results."

"Their expectations for *desired business outcome*," a manager from Chicago chimed in.

Another manager from San Francisco didn't give them a chance to continue. "Discovery is when we *identify the key players*, like potential coaches, Champions, gatekeepers, technical users, and enemies. By enemies, I meant competition." He gave a grin here. "The competition's Champion will essentially be our enemy."

Wow, they've been burned by the competition's Champion.

POTENTIAL CHAMPIONS

It's during the Discovery stage where potential Champions are identified.

Champions have influence in accounts, which gives them access to the Economic Buyer. (Later, we'll discuss champions in depth.)

A rep's ability to find a Champion starts with the rep finding and quantifying mission-critical business pain during Discovery.

Champions want to attach themselves to the solution of a major business pain. Reps need Champions to get them to the Economic Buyer, or the person within the company who has discretionary use of funds.

I wrote a simple logic chain on the whiteboard:

1. Find pain
2. Pain finds Champions
3. Champions get you to the Economic Buyer
4. The Economic Buyer has access to major funds
5. Sell big deals

The opposite is also true:

1. Don't find pain
2. No pain, no Champion
3. No Champion, no access to the Economic Buyer
4. No Economic Buyer, No access to major funds
5. Sell small deals or no deals

DISCOVERY QUESTIONS

"Let's put the Discovery stage into proper perspective," I said, and I tossed the marker to Kathleen. "Come on up, Kathleen. Remember that Discovery is *not* selling. *Discovery is investigating.* You're resisting discussing your product during Discovery so you can fully understand and confirm their pain."

I faced the whole group. "Your turn. Give good questions to Kathleen so she can write them down on the whiteboard. What questions can you ask to discover more about your potential client?"

- Why do you think this is a problem?
- Why do you think this happens?
- Why do you have to remedy this now?
- When does this occur?
- How often does this occur?
- Have you tried to remedy this previously? How?
- What company measure does this effect?
- Who is held personally accountable for this measure?
- How does this affect your people?
- Can you walk me through your current process?
- Who else is involved in the process?
- How does this affect other processes?
- Who else might this affect?
- How is this issue affecting the company?
- What else does it depend on?
- What is the company's desired business outcome?

ART OF DISCOVERY

"Now, even though you are investigating, there's an art to the customer conversation during the Discovery stage," I said as the answers slowed. "It's a give and take with the customer. A back-and-forth. Quid pro quo.

"We can't expect to walk into a meeting and barrage the customer with continual questions without us giving them some meaningful information to keep them engaged.

"You need to take whatever information the customer is giving you as you ask questions and confirm your understanding but have a keen sense of when the customer wants to hear from you."

"Jim," I said, "tell the group what the hockey saying, 'skate to the open ice' means."

"It means skating with the puck to the part of the ice where there is open space and time. Then, as you skate, constantly sensing when you're running out of time and space and passing the puck to your teammate," Jim explained.

"Same analogy applies when we are talking with customers. Take the time and space they give you to get as much information as possible but be acutely aware of when to give them some information about your product or customer success stories."

IMMERSED IN THE CUSTOMER CONVERSATION

Reps need to be *immersed in the customer conversation* during Discovery. Immersing in the customer conversation can only occur if reps are totally prepared with the base product and customer knowledge. For example, reps need to know base knowledge items below, *without thinking:*

1. The customer's use case
2. Typical pains in the use case

3. Open-ended discovery questions
4. Their unique product differentiators
5. How their product differentiators solve pain
6. Typical quantifiable value of their solution
7. Customer success stories with before and after scenarios

Without a cold proficiency of these items, the rep-customer conversation becomes mechanical, with fits of stops and starts. The rep has to think when they should be listening, thinking when they should be understanding, thinking when they should be feeling instead.

Because the rep isn't prepared, they can't totally immerse themselves in the art of the customer conversation and drive the conversation to a valuable conclusion. If they already know the answers, they can devote their attention to listening and understanding.

Being immersed in the conversation is a constant loop of four core actions:

1. Questioning:
Asking the open-ended questions
2. Listening:
Listening to understand
3. Confirming:
Verifying your complete understanding
4. Feeling:
Sensing the customers response

It was time to get into some more questions, so I turned to the room. "So, what information may the customer want to hear from us? Shannon?"

"A summary of our conversation," she said. "After summarizing, ask the customer if we understand their pain and environment correctly. Are we missing any critical information?"

"How our product capabilities align to potentially solve their pain," Carlos said, then tacked on, "and why we're different than the competition."

"My customers like to hear a few success stories where other customers had the same pain and explain how we achieved tangible results with our solution. They want to know that we've seen the problem before, and they are not the only company with the issue," Kathleen said.

I was very surprised by what I heard from them, which varied dramatically from what I had observed during the QBR and sales calls. They intuitively knew what information to discover, but they weren't doing it. Like so many immature enterprise sales-forces, they weren't truly interested in the customer's issues, they were rushing to present their product and clamoring to drive a POC.

They were taking shortcuts.

Andy spoke up, "How do we know when a rep has fulfilled the requirements of the Discovery stage? Can you give us an example of a customer verifiable exit criteria or gate?"

The brute-force expression from earlier had subsided. Andy didn't sit with his legs crossed and arms crossed over his chest anymore. Some of the glower had left his eyes.

"Of course," I said. "A gate could be sending an email to the customer that outlines all the required information and the next scheduled meeting. For example, the email verifies the discov-ered pain, the players involved, the desired business outcome, and it details the next step in the process. The rep should share the confirming email with you and calendar the customer meeting for the next stage to indicate completion of Discovery."

A flurry of typing fingers and a few rustling papers followed.

19
POC WIN RATES

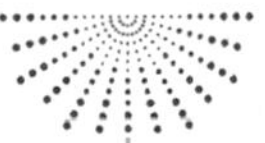

I was anxious to get to their low POC win rate because that was one of *their* major sales process issues.

"Good. I like what I'm hearing. To stress the importance of Discovery to the overall success of the sales process, I want to revisit what I heard during the QBR regarding your POC win rate." Dennis, the CRO, reminded me of their POC metrics:

- Twenty-five percent POC win rate
- Four weeks in length
- Average deal size of $50,000
- Rep quota of 1.2 million dollars

Even as I wrote those numbers on the whiteboard, my stomach started to hurt. I needed to find a way for management to understand the implications of a low POC win rate. The reps made Herculean efforts for this company, and I didn't think the management team even saw that yet.

For a second, I stared at that number, then stepped back.

"OK, so your reps have an annual quota of 1.2 million dollars. With an average new deal size of $50,000, each rep would need how many orders per year to make their number?"

Jim barked out, "Twenty-four."

That meant closing one new deal every two weeks. I whistled. "That is an extremely fast pace for an enterprise sales force to run on a consistent basis."

The low win rate made it even more difficult to successfully scale the sales force over time, which Raj had already started to realize.

"What's the average deal size for existing customers?" I asked Dennis.

"For new and existing customers, it's approximately the same, $50,000. A third of our deals come from the installed base, and the remainder from new customers where the rep needs to do a POC."

"All right." I rubbed my hands together. "Let's break that down."

The reps needed to win eighteen new customers through a POC and obtain six deals through existing customers. With a win rate of only twenty-five percent, the rep needed seventy-two POCs (18 x 4 = 72) running each year to get eighteen new customers.

Andy pulled up his calculator on his phone. "That's an average of one-and-a-half POCs per week, six POCs per month, and seventeen POCs per quarter." He shook his head. "That's way too many!"

Andy was dead right—that was a huge amount of activity. Just to make their number for the year, the rep would need to run seventy-two sales campaigns with new customers and a minimum of six campaigns with existing customers. That placed a tremendous burden on the sales reps to generate pipeline.

I asked Dennis, "How do the reps generate pipeline?"

"The reps receive about fifty percent of their qualified leads that close from Marketing, and the remainder are self-generated."

Hard to believe they get fifty percent from Marketing.

"What is the Marketing Qualified Lead (MQL) to Sales Closed conversion ratio?" I asked.

"Ten percent."

"Since the reps receive half their leads from Marketing, Marketing would need to supply how many leads to each rep?"

"Well, we just said they need to do seventy-two POCs," Jim said. Andy tapped into his calculator as Jim spoke. "Half the leads come from MQLs, so seventy-two divided by two equals thirty-six POCs generated from Marketing leads. With only a ten percent close rate, that means each rep would need Marketing to generate . . ."

"Three hundred and sixty MQLs per rep," Andy finished.

"That's an astronomical amount," Raj said.

And totally unsustainable as Raj and Dennis tried to scale the sales force.

"How are reps generating their own qualified leads that don't come from Marketing?" I asked.

"Mainly cold call and email," Andy said. "Their cold-call and email to close ratios are only ten percent, so the reps would need to self-generate another 360 qualified leads themselves. No wonder our reps complain about not getting the support they need from to generate pipeline!"

I summarized it on the whiteboard to really drive the impossibility home:

- Manage seventeen POCs per quarter
- Qualify ninety MQLs from Marketing per quarter and start eighteen sales campaigns per quarter
- Cold call and email to generate ninety qualified leads to start eight sales campaigns per quarter
- Manage the installed base of customers to generate six upsell deals during the year

There were a number of issues there, and I wrote those out as well:

- Marketing is not generating enough qualified leads
- An overwhelming burden on Sales to generate their own qualified leads
- The average deal size is small
- The POC win rate is too low
- The POC time frame is too long

"Even though all of these issues need to be addressed, the paramount issue is the low POC win rate of twenty-five percent. The low win rate combined with the average length of time for a POC is breaking the backs of your reps. Of all the issues, increasing the POC win rate would have the largest effect on your overall bookings and sales productivity numbers.

"Skipping steps early in the sales process is the core reason your win rate is low and the POC time is long. You are performing an excess amount of unqualified POCs. As you learn to increase the POC win rate by increasing your sales effectiveness, I'll wager that the number of POC's and the POC time frame will decrease."

20
RAMIFICATIONS OF SKIPPING STEPS

During the QBR session, it was difficult for me to understand why Forego sales managers continually harped on the sales reps for more activity, more activity, more activity. Their motto was activity is good. I agree that activity is good, if it's purposeful. Activity is good if it results in meaningful accomplishments—like measurable deal progression and higher POC win rates.

Activity without a deep analysis of results, without ever understanding the cause of the reps' selling problems, is meaningless.

It became clear that they were "jumping the gun," driving their reps to prematurely get to a POC, because they believed customers only bought after a POC.

In one way, they would be correct. In another way, they were entirely wrong.

"You seem stuck on the fact that your customers only buy after a POC," I said. "The problem with that premise is, only one in four customers buy after a POC. Since you are pushing reps to perform a POC, your reps don't have time to perform proper discovery or quantification of the customer pain.

"Your focus needs to completely change. Today, you have a self-centered product sales focus. Your reps need to have an authentic sales focus on the buyer."

"Your reps aren't focused on understanding the problem you solve for customers. They never understand the pain in the customer's environment, the customer's business goals and the alignment of your product capabilities to their pains. They never understand if the customer is buying what they're selling."

A POC should only occur late in the sales process.

But when reps are measured only on POC activity, they give the transactional, scorekeeper manager exactly what they want. More POC's. Not high quality POC's, just more POC's. To get more POC's, they skip steps in the early stages of the process.

In turn, skipping steps results in the customer never understanding the entire value of your product and because you don't go through a process, rarely will the customer understand the magnitude of their pain.

It's a blind exchange.

The customer is blind to your unique product capabilities, and the rep is blind to the customer's pain.

Forego faced several negative ramifications to skipping steps in the sales process.

1. SMALL DEAL SIZES

Skipping steps leads to small deal sizes. Your sales team is only selling features and functions. They don't understand the pains they're solving for customers or the tangible benefits customers get from your product.

Customers buy the benefit they get from your product, not the product itself.

There's the old example of the hole and the drill bit. Customers buy a half-inch drill bit for the benefit of getting a half-inch hole in a piece of wood. They don't buy the drill bit for its features.

In the twenty-five percent of Forego's cases in which an account actually purchased after a POC, their sales reps had been lucky to get an intelligent customer on the phone. The smart customer listened to the features (the drill bit features) and functions (how the bit works with the drill), and mentally performed a "back of the napkin" cost justification.

The familiar scenario goes something like this: After the customer does their quick cost justification, the customer asks, "How much does the product cost?" The rep, anxious to sell a deal, gives the customer a price far below the cost justification the customer calculated. And certainly, far below the total potential business value of the solution.

The customer gave the rep what they asked for—a "Hobson's choice," a take-it-or-leave-it deal. Small dollars.

Trapped, and anxious to sell a deal, the rep takes it.

Loose change.

Meaningless.

Many reps believe customers buy products based on price. What they need to learn is that *customers buy products based on the value they perceive they will receive,* not price.

2. THE CUSTOMER IS LOW IN THE ORGANIZATION.

When your rep sells features and functions, they aren't selling business solutions that create tangible and lasting value for a company.

The person buying for features and functions is low in the organization. A small cog in the wheel. They don't have access to major funds to influence a deal with a large price point.

Because the rep is solely focused on whiz-bang product features instead of business issues, they never gain access to people high in the account, who are oriented toward operating the business. If, by chance, they try selling features and functions high in an organization, they quickly get relegated to lower levels of the account to people who deal with low level issues. Anyone with experience knows, "you get relegated to whom they sound like"

3. HIGH PROBABILITY OF DEAL "CHURN."

Forego sold a SaaS-subscription product that renewed annually. Customers may not renew their subscription if they don't receive tangible value for the product. If they originally gave you "loose change" for some of your features and functions, never understanding the full business value of your product capabilities, then when budgets get cut, the products with the lowest perceived business value get cut first.

No business value, no renewal.

No renewal, account churn.

4. INACCURATE FORECAST.

The ability of the leadership team to produce an accurate forecast each quarter is next to impossible when steps are skipped.

The impact, in Forego's case, would only worsen as Forego tried to scale the sales force. For example, Forego had 50 reps running 17 POCs, which meant the company ran 850 POCs per quarter. The 25-percent win rate produced 212 wins, but *638* losses!

Good luck creating an accurate forecast when you lose 75 percent of your POCs every quarter.

5. REP ATTRITION RATES INCREASE

Remember, when you measure your reps on activities only, without ever understanding specifically why they fail or succeed, you are nothing more than a glorified scorekeeper. Your reps are never trained to gain insight into the sales process, and their skills are never developed.

Your reps feel like gerbils on a wheel. They feel disrespected. Disrespect leads to rep attrition, and Forego's attrition stood at thirty-five percent.

21

SLOW DOWN TO GO FAST

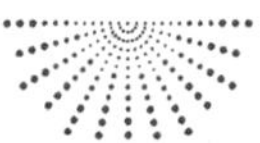

When reps rush through the sales process knowing little-to-nothing about the customer's environment, how can they practically convince the customer that their product solves their pain? They can't. Without that knowledge, they can't possibly set the success criteria for the POC.

"It's time to teach the reps to *slow down to go fast*," I said. "Have them slow down during the first two stages of the sales process. That ensures an understanding of the magnitude of the customer's pains and environment, which in turn can translate to a potential match to your product."

From near the back, Kathleen raised her hand. "Many times, customers push us to go faster," she said. "They make demands. They push *us* for a POC, either to respond to an RFP or to just give them a price quote."

"When you speak to them, are you typically speaking to a high-level executive?"

She laughed. "No."

"Right. Most of the time, it's a lower-level person. And in the majority of cases, the person demanding the POC is no more prepared to articulate the magnitude of their pains than any person you happen to cold-call. Do they fully comprehend why the company has to buy?"

"No."

"Or why the company needs to buy now?"

"No."

"Do they know why your product may be the best fit to solve their specific issue?"

"No"

"Or how your product is differentiated from the competition?"

"Definitely not."

"So why rush through the process? Why would anyone want to be a sales rep that blindly performs POCs and simply sends out price quotes with only a hope of obtaining an order?"

Her expression turned thoughtful. I remembered her presentation in the QBR. No doubt, her deals would have massively benefitted from slowing down the process, and I could tell she knew it.

GET "ABOVE THE NOISE"

Shannon and I had gone on a call to a company named First Data and had come out with a beautiful example of how high-level buyers focus on solving major business issues. It was the perfect reason to show why Forego needed to discover big business pains.

"Shannon." I called for her with a wave of my hand. "Come on up and tell the team about our experience at First Data."

She agreed and stood next to me in front of the sales managers.

"We met with the CIO and CISO," she explained with her slight Irish burr. "I wanted to know what issues would gain the attention of C-level executives. So, I decided to ask them, 'how do you deal with all of the vendors and make sense of all the different products salespeople are trying to sell to you?'

"He said, 'We deal with thousands of vendors selling thousands of products, especially in the security world where there is a plethora of choices. We have hundreds of issues to solve, but only the vendors who focus on solving the largest problems our company faces obtain our business.

"He continued, 'Let me give you an analogy. Most internal and external people *think* I'm a firefighter. But I'm *actually* a forest ranger. I overlook millions and millions of acres of land. My job is to think of the long-term safety of our people, our intellectual property, and potential threats that could affect the entire land mass. That means I can't put out all the fires. Some fires will burn. Let them burn. I have to focus on preventing and extinguishing the largest fires that threaten our company.'

"Then he looked straight at me and said, 'Shannon, every company has fires, most of which they can live with. If you want to sell high in an organization, get *above the noise.*'" Her voice quieted slightly here. "That's a saying I won't forget. 'Above the noise.'"

A few moments of thoughtful silenced passed.

"Interesting," Jim said, "because companies live with hundreds of pains that aren't negatively impacting the cost for them to run their business. In many of our deals, customers bought for small dollars for the few small pains that we discovered."

At the highest levels of an organization, business pain is related to revenue, profitability, and risk. As you move down the organization, the words may change, the measures change, but it is how those measures translate to revenue, profitability, and risk, that gets you above the noise.

COMMON PAIN AREAS

Together, we grouped a few common company pain areas that sales managers could teach their reps to look for.

1. **Regulation:** Non-compliance to regulatory issues like PCI SSC (Payment Card Industry), HIPAA (Health Insurance Portability and Accountability Act of 1996) and GDPR-General Data Protection Regulation.
2. **Competition:** Continual improvements in their processes to maintain a competitive edge. They may need to move their IT infrastructure and applications to the cloud to meet or beat their competition.
3. **Security***:* The move to multiple cloud vendors, mobile devices, work from home initiatives, AI, and machine learning implementations can cause potential opening for cyber-attacks.
4. **Productivity, Cost, and Quality:** Process and operational pain from ongoing business activities, procedures, processes, labor and systems may cause lost productivity, inflict higher costs, and create quality issues.
5. **Reputation:** Unhappy customers or product failures can negatively impact a company's brand on social media, causing reputational risk.

22
SCOPING

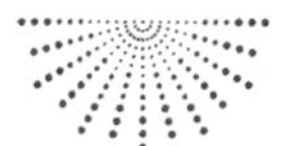

Scoping is the second step of a B2B Sales Process. During the Scoping stage, reps take the pain uncovered during Discovery to *quantify and implicate that pain.*

"Reps need to quantify the metrics surrounding the customer's current *as-is* process and to define the preliminary metrics of a *to-be* process," I said to the room. "With this information, they've gained an intimate understanding of how things are done today and how they will operate in the future."

"Why do we need to know both the *as-is* and *to-be* processes?" Kathleen asked.

I held out my hands. "Anyone want to answer Kathleen?"

"Because later we'll use the *before and after* metrics to present a cost justification," Jim said. "The cost justification will help during price negotiations to increase our average deal size."

"Understanding the *to-be* process, and their associated business outcome, helps us understand why they have to buy," Carlos said.

"Without quantified pain," Andy said, "there is no way to prove business value, so there is only small deals, no large deals."

"In simple terms, Andy means that *in the cost justification, the customer's gain must be significantly larger than the customer's pain*. It's the only way to prove value and get a large deal. That's why our customers gave us small deals since the value they perceived was minor," said Jim.

Jim glanced at Andy, and I felt a moment of tension in my neck. Would Andy take exception to Jim speaking for him? Instead of reacting with annoyance or a flare of anger, Andy simply nodded.

They were exactly right. Not quantifying the before and after is the main reason so many salespeople can't overcome price objections. The customer won't magically understand the value of your product.

I went on, "From now on, I want you to stop saying POC and start saying POV, Proof of Value. Proof of Concept is pointless. Your product works. You're not trying to prove the concept of your technology functioning. What is important is that you can prove that your product capabilities deliver business value to the customer for their specific use case."

"That forces us to change our mindset *from proving technology to proving value*, POC versus POV," said Carlos.

"That's the right mindset, Carlos."

"We'll also need to *implicate the pain*," Jim said, seeming a little relieved himself. "We need to understand the negative consequences of the customer *not* solving the problem now."

"And we need to know *who suffers and what suffers*," the Chicago manager said. "Which person in the organization is most impacted by the pain, and which company measure will suffer the most. Then it's easier to understand to whom we have to sell."

Only during the Scoping stage can the sales force acquire a deep understanding of the customer environment. Many great reps share their sales process with the customer.

They outline three major parts to the Scoping journey:

1. **Scoping:** A method to understand and quantify their business pain and outline a potential POV. (The method will decide if there is alignment between product capabilities and pain, between seller capabilities and customer value.)
2. **A Go/No-Go Meeting:** A meeting with the Economic Buyer to confirm whether or not the pain is a priority to solve
3. **The POV:** The outline of the POV criteria, incorporating the required product capabilities and timeframe for a POV

The Scoping journey will generate three documents for review:

1. **A Cost Justification** with *as-is* and *to-be* metrics
2. **A POV Plan** that directly correlates to the POV criteria and preliminary cost justification
3. **A Preliminary Pricing Proposal** which is a price quote is based upon the preliminary cost justification

This journey can only happen *early* in a sales process (which is why reps should slow down). This is the time to garner as much knowledge as possible for the rep to gain control of the deal.

If you wait too long to gather this information, the sale creeps into the later stages of the sales process, where there is a *dynamic shift* in which the customer can discern the capabilities of your product.

With that understanding, the customer becomes more reluctant to share pain and process metrics. When the customer has connected the dots between their problem and your solution, they no longer require anything more from you than pricing information.

"As you look back at your past deals," I asked them, "what were the negative ramifications of moving too fast through these first critical stages?"

"Our low POC—I mean POV—win rates and low average deal sizes are caused by us not taking enough time to discover all the pains," Carlos said. He mumbled under his breath a little bit and began again. "We're too anxious to present. Too thrilled to find any pain. Once we find any—even a small pain—we stop investigating and pitch our product. Since we start presenting too soon, most times we don't find the biggest pain, and we certainly never find all the pains."

"It's why we struggle to justify our price point," Shannon said. "We never quantify all the pains into a cost justification proving value. We end up with small deal sizes. We leave money on the table."

"Keeps us from high levels, too," Hannlin said. "Executives aren't interested in our product's features and functions. They want to solve major business issues. They are looking for significant business value, and they won't find it in our features and functions."

"No wonder I can't find Champions," Kathleen muttered. "I never understand the business implications of not solving the pain. What potential Champion would care if we don't seem to be offering the solution they need? It's why we wind up with low-level coaches."

I stepped back and watched the discussion unfold.

It was almost like they didn't even need me anymore.

23
"BOX UP"

A great salesperson I knew sold a commodity product with no competitive differentiation. Yet, he found a way to engage prospects with the right questions to quickly uncover, quantify, and implicate pain.

While busy in my small office in Lexington, MA, one night around 6:00 p.m., I sat in an uncomfortable office chair behind a cheap particleboard desk with a Formica laminate top.

Just off a call with a rep from Chicago, my phone rang. Thinking it could be someone on my sales team, I quickly answered.

"This is John."

"John, it's Dan from Northwestern Mutual. How are you doing?"

I thought, *Ah, damn. The last thing I need now is to listen to a sales pitch from an insurance rep.*

"Dan, I'm fine but I don't have time to hear a sales pitch on life insurance."

As if he'd expected my objection, he responded, "Listen, John, from one salesperson to another, just give me five minutes to ask you a few questions."

Remembering all the cold calls I had made in my sales career; I felt a little empathy. "All right. Shoot."

That's when Dan asked, "Do you have any children, John?"

"Two. A boy who's five and a girl who's seven."

"Are you planning to put the kids through college?"

"Yes, Dan. For sure."

"How much do you think it will cost for each child to attend college?"

"Two hundred fifty thousand each, probably."

At this point, Dan definitely had me thinking of my kids. On one hand, I was wary of revealing too much personal information over the phone to some stranger.

On the other hand, I was *curious* to learn his call strategy.

"Do you own a home?" he asked.

"Yes."

"How much is your mortgage?"

"I owe an awful lot of money on my mortgage," I said with a failing chuckle. My house was a gamble. I'd leveraged my finances, counting on working hard and making enough money in the future to pay for it, but things could always get bleak fast.

"Does your wife work?"

"No."

"If she did work, how much money could she earn?"

I laughed to myself, then replied, "Not enough to pay the bills."

"Enough to pay the mortgage?"

"No."

"Do you spend a lot of money every month?"

"All I really own is a watch, a bicycle, and a car. My wife and kids own everything else."

We both laughed. Between the lines, I could tell that Dan was building a cost justification. He knew the money hot spots and was quantifying the major costs in my life.

But he still went further.

"Do you have any parents or in-laws in the area?" he asked.

"No, I married a Dutch woman. All of her family is in the Netherlands, and my parents passed away."

Then, Dan switched gears. "Now, John, if you '*box up*' tomorrow, what would happen?"

"What do you mean, 'box up'?"

Dan showed some empathy here, which softened the macabre approach. "I know it's tough to imagine what happens when you die, when they put you in a box and drop you six feet into the earth. But think of it this way, if you 'box up' tomorrow, would your wife have to go back to work?"

"Yes, I guess so."

"Is it possible your wife would have to sell the house, because she can't pay the mortgage?"

He already knew the answer, of course. I started to get anxious. I could feel the answers I gave him come back at me like a giant trap. It was closing fast, and there wasn't a way out.

"Yes, that most likely would have to happen," I said.

"Would your wife have to put your kids in a daycare center since she has to work?"

I knew what he was doing, but I was still curious to hear the rest of his strategy.

"Of course."

"Since you have no relatives in the area, who would drop off and pick up your kids from daycare every day if your wife is working?"

I definitely hadn't thought about that. Now thinking about the future of my kids was uncomfortable.

Now, I couldn't think about anything *but* this conversation.

"And, if you did 'box up,' have you considered that your kids wouldn't be able to attend college?"

Now, I wondered how I could be so stupid not to have life insurance.

What would happen to my family if I was hit by a bus on the way home from work?

At this point, Dan had changed my priority on life insurance from never considering it to a must-have, top-priority purchase.

Dan created urgency.

I needed insurance.

I needed it NOW.

So, I did it—I bought the life insurance from Dan. And learned a few great lessons in the meantime.

24
TARGET CUSTOMERS

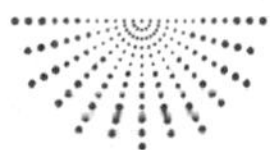

"That's a classic story," Andy said with unusual camaraderie. "Dan was a salesperson selling a product with no differentiation. Yet he knew to target you with powerful discovery and quantification questions. And he knew how to drive urgency with implication questions." He chewed on his lower lip for a second.

"That's a cool story, but we've been told, many times, that every company could buy our product. Why would we target specific customers?" asked Carlos.

"Let me answer it this way," I said. "How many of you have heard of the famous bank robber Jesse James, who carried out thirty-four bank robberies in the 1800s?"

All the hands rose.

"What was Jesse's answer when he was asked, 'Why do you rob banks?'"

Quiet filled the air while I waited to share the answer. "Jesse James said, 'Because that's where the money is!'" I howled. "He could have robbed houses, stores, trains or stagecoaches, but he chose banks, because that's where the James Gang's capabilities yielded the highest return for their effort.

"It's the same in Sales. You can speak to all the companies in the world or target the companies that will benefit most from the value of your product capabilities to generate the highest average deal sizes for you."

"What's the best way for us to do that?" asked Andy.

"It's hard work," I said. "But you should build an Ideal Customer Profile. An ICP highlights the customer pains, use cases, the personas owning the use cases, and companies with those specific use cases. It also describes the linkage between your product differentiators and the pains in the customer use cases, resulting in the quantifiable customer value received. By now, I think you inherently know most of the answers, but let's build the flow of and ideal customer profile together."

After grabbing my dry-erase marker, I turned to the room and asked, "What should we start with?"

Not surprisingly, Jim spoke up first. "A list of our unique and defensible product differentiators."

"Great."

"Then we need to map the pain points they solve for customers," Andy said.

"OK, what's next?"

I could feel them grasping for the answer, so I helped. "You'll need to align those pain points to specific customer use cases."

After I wrote that down, Hannlin leaned back, hands stacked casually behind his head, and said, "We should quantify the tangible business benefits of solving pains for each use case."

"Fantastic. What else?"

Again, the group struggled, so I shared the entire process on the board:

1. Create a list of unique and defensible product differentiators.
2. Target pain points that the differentiators solve.
3. Map pain points to specific use cases.
4. Quantify the business benefits of solving pains in each use case.
5. List the negative consequences of customers not solving the pain.
6. Discover companies/industries which have those specific uses cases.
7. List the specific personas that own those use cases.
8. Prioritize companies and industries based on highest customer value.

UNIQUE PRODUCT DIFFERENTIATORS

What are the unique differentiators of your product?
Unique differentiators are product capabilities that are unique to your product only.

DEFENSIBLE DIFFERENTIATORS

Are your unique product differentiators defensible?
In a head-to-head test of your product versus all other competitors, can you prove that your product capabilities are unique?

PAIN POINTS

What are the specific pains that your unique product differentiators solve for customers?
What does a typical company currently do to avoid or work around the pains?
Do they need additional people to complete the same task that your unique product differentiators automate?
Do they take more time to complete the tasks that your product automates?

QUANTIFIABLE BUSINESS VALUE

Can you quantify the associated business value created by your solution?
At the highest level, how does solving the problem increase revenues, decrease costs, decrease risk, or improve productivity?
Here are a few examples to discover your product's quantifiable business value:

- Does it increase revenues because they can release new applications and changes to those applications at a faster rate to their customers?
- If so, quantify the value of revenues to application changes.
- Does it decrease costs because the time to test applications is reduced?
- If so, quantify the decreased cost to test times.
- Do they need less people in the testing process to release applications?
- If so, how will it make the people they have more productive?

- Will your software help them decrease churn risk because more customers will renew their application subscription?
- If so, how many more customers will renew versus churn?

NEGATIVE CONSEQUENCES

What are the negative consequences of the customer not solving their pain?
Who suffers, or what else in the company suffers, because the pain is not alleviated?
If customers only manually test applications prior to release, does the quality of the application suffer?
Will customers reject using the application, resulting in company revenues decrease?
Will customer support be inundated with angry customer calls?
Will the company-customer churn rate increase?

USE CASES

What are the specific use cases for your product?
How are your current customers using the product?
Which use cases drive the largest quantifiable benefit to customers?

BUYERS

Which person or persons in the company would buy your product?
What are their job performance measures?

What are that person's typical priorities?
How much power do they have in the company?
What is the typical budget for your buyer?
What language do they speak?

ENVIRONMENTAL AND INFRASTRUCTURE

Are there specific prerequisite items a company must have before they would buy your product?
For instance, does your company need a potential customer to have a specific number or type of device before it makes sense to use your product? (Examples: Does the company need to have at least 500 servers, at least fifty sales reps, or spend at least two percent on marketing?)

INDUSTRY SEGMENTS AND COMPANY SIZE

Does it make sense to call on specific industry segments or companies of a specific size?

COMPANY SUPPORT

On paper, it may make sense to target a larger company or specific industry segment, but your company may not have the resources and processes to support those customers.

Dan knew everything about my persona and my situation when he called to sell me insurance. To effectively converse with their target customers, Forego needed to know everything about their target personas. Things like their title, their boss, their budget, their uses cases, their job measures, daily operating issues, people reporting to them, and their monthly or quarterly operating rhythms.

Forego needed to prioritize their top ICP targets based on those companies that would receive the *largest business value* from their solutions.

25
PROPENSITY TO BUY AND SALES COMPLEXITY

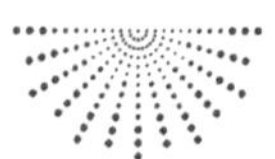

PROPENSITY TO BUY

The prioritized list of ideal customers for Forego was a good starting point for Forego to finding companies to target, but there were additional steps to consider. For instance, matching the prioritized list of companies against factors that made some companies have a *higher propensity to buy* than other companies.

Not all companies in an ICP will have the same propensity to buy. For the cloud-based software that Forego sold, they might factor a target company's propensity to buy based on several possible considerations (examples):

1. Short product life cycles.
2. "All in" on the cloud (no apps on premise).
3. The company hires the best software developers.
4. The company always purchases leading-edge technologies.
5. They must comply to new pending industry regulations.

6. Critical "impending" events

After completing the prioritized ICP list, financial service companies and federal government agencies may be at the top of the list. They might meet the ICP criteria due to large pain points, alignment of product capability, and tangible business value. But once you've factored the propensity to buy, those companies might be deprioritized on your list of top companies to initially target.

I asked the room, "Why do you think that is?"

"In my experience, financial services companies and government agencies typically have long product life cycles," Jim said with a shrug. "They're not all in on the cloud, they aren't known for hiring the world's best developers, and they're usually one of the last organizations to use cutting-edge technologies."

Andy cleared his throat and spoke up. "That's true, if you look at financial services companies in a monolithic sense. But there may be divisions or pockets inside financial services companies that may meet our ICP criteria. Like a wealth management team or the commercial banking team building an app."

SALES COMPLEXITY

"What about sales complexity?" I asked Andy, startled to find him engaging so proactively. The sullen man from earlier had mostly faded. His more inclusive language—*we* instead of *I*—was a good sign.

"Most large financial services companies and government agencies also have the most sales complexity," he said. "Many times, there are multiple decisionmakers at multiple levels in multiple locations. Access to C-level executives is difficult. Those types of companies are renowned for long evaluation timeframes, as well as the onerous size and scope of their legal paperwork."

Jim added, "Reps take a significant beating during the lengthy procurement and legal process in those companies. Since we only have 50 sales reps, the combination of low propensity to buy, and high sales complexity will make us push financial services companies and government agencies further down on our prioritization list."

A wide range of companies in an ICP list meant that some would have more complexity in their processes and organizational structure, making the selling effort longer and more complex.

I listed a few different degrees of selling complexity for deliberation:

- Multiple-stakeholder decision
- Multi-Level decision
- Multi-Department decision
- Multi-Location decision
- Accessibility to C-level executives.
- Lengthy POV requirement
- Strong cost-justification hurdles
- Lengthy Legal and Procurement processes

I set the dry-erase marker back down. They were *really* starting to get it now.

"Those are the high-level steps to building an ICP," I said. "It's hard work, but it pays off to know your target customers, the key personas, specific use cases, and major pain points before you make a sales call. It's the only way to effectively converse with your customer."

"Can we go back to the 'box up' story?" Andy asked.

I nodded for him to continue, and he kept speaking.

"Dan's power lay in his questions, which he built off of his ideal customer profile. His questions were so targeted and precise that he never presented his product. He understood your pains, desires, and vulnerabilities.

"He truly *implicated pain by creating a negative outcome that focused on problems and the potential fear of not solving those problems.* That forced you to reevaluate your purchase priorities. That is what we need to do."

Which led me right to my next point.

26
LEADING THE WITNESS

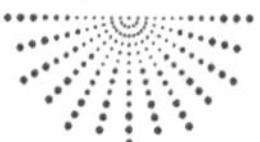

In the Discovery and Scoping stages, great salespeople imitate great lawyers.

The best lawyers lead their witness through carefully crafted questions. Their main goal is to get the witness, through meticulous questioning, to admit to certain things. They're very precise with their questions. They typically won't ask one if they don't suspect an expected or desired answer.

A great lawyer is also well prepared with questions pertinent to the witness and their current situations. They assess the witnesses' personas, know their daily lives, and understand their common pains and worries.

Most importantly, they intently listen to the witnesses' answers. Through careful listening, they ask secondary and tertiary questions to garner additional pertinent information to build their case.

Remember, the ability to be "immersed in the customer conversation" is due to complete and total preparation. Meaning, without hesitation, they understand the customer's use case and know how their product differentiation leads to a potential valuable solution for the customer.

* * *

"I DIDN'T KNOW it at the time," I said, "but Dan did his homework before he called me. He spoke to my financial advisor. He looked me up on LinkedIn. He knew where I worked and where I lived, how many kids I had, and approximately how much money I made.

"I was his ideal target customer with a high propensity to buy. A married, working professional with two young kids, a non-working wife, a large mortgage, and a high monthly burn rate."

Like a good lawyer, Dan had selected precisely crafted *discovery* questions for which he knew the expected answer:

- How many kids do you have?
- Does your wife work?
- Do you have a mortgage?

Then, Dan dug in, asking the *quantification* questions:

- How much will college cost?
- How much is your mortgage?
- How much money do you spend every month?

Finally, he moved to *implicate* the pain. Helped me to understand negative consequences I'd never considered. He never presented his product. Never directly told me what would happen if I "boxed up." He just asked what he already knew.

He made me "feel" the pain and woke me from my *positive current state*—unawareness of my pain—into the realization of a *negative current state*. And he did all that with implication questions:

- What happens if you die?
- What happens to the mortgage on the house?
- Will your wife have to go back to work?
- Who will pick up the kids from day care?
- Will the kids ever be able to get a college education?

His precise *questions formulated pain into fear*. The fear of a potential *negative future state*. Fear of a possible negative reality. Fear of the unknown.

Fear was a robust motivator for me to change my priorities and buy insurance.

Insurance of a *positive future outcome*.

There was no sale when he only identified my pain. And potentially no sale after he quantified my pain. There was only a sale when he started to implicate the pain. He created an *urgency for me to move from my current state of pain to a positive future outcome*.

"I want to clarify one thing," I said to the room. "The Dan story is a classic example of leading the witness. Certainly, Dan did his homework and knew me allowing him to ask precision questions —many of which were *closed ended,* since he could predict the range of my answers. And he sold a commodity product. At Forego, you sell a complex software product which requires you to ask pinpoint *open-ended* questions and then listen carefully to dig deeper.

"Some salespeople will find pain, but fewer salespeople quantify pain, and only a small minority will ever implicate pain," I continued. "If salespeople never quantify pain, they can't justify their price point. If salespeople never implicate pain, they never create urgency. They never give the customer a powerful reason to buy *now*. A reason for them to change their priorities. That's why so many forecasted deals die a slow death."

"Time kills all deals without urgency. If you haven't established urgency, then, as time moves on, the customer believes they can continue to operate without your solution."

I circled back to the logic chain we'd built on the whiteboard earlier. "Let's wrap up Scoping by adding to this."

1. Found business pain creates opportunity.
2. Quantified business pain drives higher price points.
3. Implicated business pain drives urgency.
4. Business pain and urgency finds business Champions.
5. Business champions get you to the Economic Buyer.
6. The Economic Buyer has access to major funds.
7. You sell big deals based on value.

The opposite is also true:

1. No discovered pain means a small or no opportunity.
2. No quantified business pain means no cost justification.
3. No implicated business pain means no urgency to buy.
4. No business Champion means no access to the Economic Buyer.
5. No access to the Economic Buyer means no access to major funds.
6. No access to major funds means either selling small deals based on product features or selling no deals.

At this point, their glassy-eyed expressions meant it was time for a break. I'd packed their heads full of enough for them to get started implementing change, even though we'd only gone through two steps of the B2B sales process.

"Look, it's time to take a break," I said, and turned to Raj and Dennis. "This is enough for now. Your sales managers can work with the reps on what they've learned, and you'll start to see changes in your sales force as it rolls out. Before I let you go, let's finalize Scoping with one question. Jim, what is a gate for the Scoping stage? What customer verifiable events need to occur for you to know when your reps have finished Scoping?"

"When we have a full understanding of the *customer pains* and *how our capabilities align to the pain*. You need to know that they're buying what you're selling, as well as the *negative consequences of them not solving their pain*."

Jim, with his already-excellent leaderships skills, had taken a step onto the path. He was beginning to understand where to go next, and that was a great thing to see. There was still a lot of implementation to be performed, but I was happy to see him appear more confident.

"There will also be a quantification of pain in a *cost justification* based on the *as-is* and *to-be* processes," Hannlin said.

"We'll have to *find a Champion*, too," Andy said. "If we don't have a Champion, there's no sense in moving any further down the sales process."

"That's exactly right, and we'll discuss how you find and attract Champions a little later," I said. "Now, let's take a dinner break. I've given you enough today for you to teach your teams about the Discovery and Scoping stage. I'm going on sales calls with some of you to help you implement these items. For the rest of you, I'll see you next quarter."

27

Q & A WITH THE MANAGERS

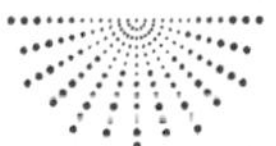

After clearing out of the conference room, we walked to Smith's Bar on Forty-Fourth and Eighth. Smith's old neon sign had lit the outside of the bar since 1954, before it went out of business in 2015. A retired New York firefighter took over Smith's and turned the bar's operations around and its legendary neon sign back on.

After a long day inside the conference room, I couldn't wait to get outside and be in a different place.

The walk over gave me a few minutes to process the day. From that session, Andy had morphed. Instead of defensiveness, a bulldog attitude, and a general uncertainty regarding Jim, he seemed open. He tried to learn. He'd grabbed at information he could use to quickly implement for himself and his team. He seemed to really care about changing his ways to help his team.

Jim had moved from being uncertain to being a great deal more confident. Now he had a path pointing in a direction he could believe in, and he wanted to walk on it. Both of them *wanted* to do better for their team. Now that they knew *what* to do, their demeanors had totally changed.

After some small talk while we ordered, Andy said, "We have some more questions after today. Mind if we ask?"

"Go ahead."

"We discussed the ICP and targeting companies with the highest propensity to buy, but, as sales leaders, what are the major components that go into maximizing our team's productivity?"

"Every quarter, the main measure of success for a sales leader at any level is your bookings number relative to your plan or, if you sell a consumption-based SaaS product, it's your product revenue relative to plan."

"If we start at the top," I said as everyone else leaned in to hear better. A sales leader only has two things to produce bookings (or revenues):

People
Productivity

The number of people you have is usually determined by your CEO and CFO, leaving you with the responsibility of maintaining the people on your team and increasing the productivity of your team. Every year, your CEO and CFO build a productivity model consisting of three main components:

1. **Ramp Time** for new reps (Usually six months for enterprise reps).
2. **Average Sales Productivity** of the sales force.
3. **Rep Attrition** (Usually twenty percent for enterprise reps. This number includes promotions from rep to manager).

Those components will dictate the annual quota assigned to you. If those are your major quota components and we simplify how to beat quota, your overall focus should be:

To beat Ramp Time
Recruit only A players.
Provide excellent onboarding training
Develop rep skills through on-the-job coaching to make them productive *before their defined ramp* time ends.

To increase Average Sales Productivity
Recruit A Players
Provide constant ongoing training and skill development.
Match the skillset of your reps to their target accounts.
Maintain consistent pipeline generation of qualified prospects.
Analyze and monitor deal advancement issues.

To lower Rep Attrition
Recruit A players
Understand each reps' strengths and weaknesses.
Coach effectively to help them personally grow and win deals.
Know when to manage and when to lead.

RECRUITING DEFINES YOU

"I need to recruit another sales rep," Jim said after swallowing the last bite of a juicy burger. "From your perspective, why is recruiting so important?"

"Your ability to recruit will determine your success as a manager," I said. "It's the greatest factor in determining your team's performance, and, potentially, your career. If you're a great recruiter or a lousy recruiter, recruiting will define you."

The following statement isn't 100% true, but I want to emphasize this to put the importance of recruiting in perspective:

If sales managers hire C-grade players and do everything else perfectly—onboarding, training, developing, and maintaining a great sales process—that team will still have a difficult time becoming the number one sales force. However, if you hire only grade A players and do everything else average, the A players will help you find a way to win.

Now, I'm not advocating doing everything average, but I am stressing the importance of focusing on finding and recruiting only grade A players.

WHAT TO LOOK FOR IN A RECRUIT?

"I can get behind that," Jim said. "I've seen *A* and *C* players in my time. But what criteria separates them?"

"There's a criterion that separates the As from the Bs and Cs, but the major factor in recruiting them is the sales leader."

There's a saying that, *"A* leaders recruit *A* reps and *B* leaders recruit *C* reps."

"Why is that?" asked Andy

"A leaders are secure in their abilities as leaders and only want the best people. *B* leaders are insecure in their abilities and afraid that if they recruit an *A*, the *A* may jeopardize their position as a leader.

Thinking that recruiting As will jeopardize your position is wrong thinking. As will only make you look like a great leader."

There are four major categories to consider for any prospective candidate. As we discuss these, you should build a *position description*, which defines these categories for your specific sales process and the stage of your companys' growth.

Position Description Categories:

Knowledge
Skills
Characteristics
Execution Experience

KNOWLEDGE AND SKILLS

It's important to look for people who possess the knowledge, the WHAT TO DO, and skills, the HOW TO DO IT, to be successful in your particular sales process. The knowledge and skills required for your sales process may be quite different than the sales process requirements for other SaaS companies.

If there's not a direct alignment between the required skills and knowledge of the candidate and your sales process, then you're *taking a large risk* in hiring that candidate. If you can't cover their deficiencies with knowledge training and skill development, then hiring them is a complete risk. For instance, do you have a training class to increase their knowledge? Do you have a leader that can increase their skill deficiency will good coaching?

As we walk through each stage of the sales process, you should *incorporate the knowledge and skill requirements for each stage of your sales process* into the position description.

SKILLSET MATCH TO TARGET ACCOUNTS

"But why is it so important to match the skillset of the rep to their target accounts?" Jim asked. "Shouldn't anybody be able to get into any account."

"Sure, many reps may be able to get into certain accounts, but they may not have the required skills to network and sell within those accounts. Remember, we discussed the different levels of sales complexity in accounts."

I shared this analogy: Tom Brady may be remembered as one of the greatest football players to ever play the game.

As a quarterback, Tom Brady has tremendous *knowledge about the game* of football, but he would absolutely fail if he tried to play any other position other than quarterback. Tom might have an intense knowledge of the game, but he *doesn't have the skillset to play any other position* on the field.

This analogy applies to Sales.

You can't just hire people who know sales. For reps to be successful within their target accounts, you have to choose each rep based on whether or not they have the required skillset. You have to place them into the appropriate accounts that match their skills or the player will fail.

Classic mistake.

I once worked with a company named Puck.

Puck sold a general-purpose BI solution. It was a complex sale that required a rep to do pain discovery on multiple use cases with multiple stakeholders across multiple departments. The rep had to understand and manage varying requirements from different personas and then have the skill to get those different buyers to agree on a single solution from Puck that could meet their needs.

A new CEO arrived and decided to hire only people from his last company, which sold an HR solution, where reps called on one specific person in one department for one specific use case.

Not having thought through the huge difference in skillsets required by a rep to sell Puck, versus a single-threaded HR solution, caused the company to fail miserably quarter after quarter.

Eventually, the company was sold for assets.

You'll need to match the skills of the candidate to the complexity of the sales process at the target account. For instance, maybe a rep can handle a multi-stakeholder sale, where they called on multiple people in a small company or single department, but they've never dealt with the complexities of multiple stakeholders, at multiple levels, and across multiple departments.

In a multi-stakeholder, multi-level, multi-department sale, you might see added complexities to the sales process:

1. Different departmental requirements making it difficult to lock down a common decision criteria
2. Different messaging to different stakeholders at different levels
3. The need to discover and build multiple Champions in multiple departments
4. The difficulty of driving a single decision process across stakeholders in multiple departments
5. Budgeting complexities for different departments or business units
6. The difficulty of building cost justifications to meet the needs of each department

"OK, that makes perfect sense," Andy said. "We need to build a position description, which matches the knowledge and skills in our sales process to the candidate's knowledge and skills. Then for account assignments, ensure that we match our reps' skillsets to their target accounts."

"Yes, Andy. You can teach knowledge and develop skills, but I'd like you to consider one important element of recruiting, you'll never change the person's character. That's why *character is the difference maker.*"

RECRUITING CHARACTER

I have to tell you a story on recruiting the character of a person:

There were times when it was the correct look and protocol, no matter where in the world, for candidates to show up clean shaven, in a suit and tie, for an interview. This was especially true in Italy where sophisticated style and a natural elegance are inherent cultural traits. Most Italians I interviewed showed up in their Brioni, Giorgio Armani, Ermenegildo Zegna, or Canali suits. They'd be clean shaven, their hair slicked back with some product, and strutting in an expensive pair of Salvatore Ferragamo shoes.

This one man was uncharacteristically like anyone else I had ever interviewed, in any country, when he showed up in my Milano, Italy office.

He walked in with a three-day-old beard, a closely cropped, DIY haircut, and a black turtleneck sweater covered with a purple sports jacket. In addition, his tan corduroy pants with large, tufted cords and brown shoes were atypical of any Italian candidate I had previously met. It was hard to understand his broken-English answers, and I couldn't help noticing his two chipped front teeth when he smiled.

It was in the initial minute of meeting Carlo Carpanelli when I had these mixed thoughts of "who sent this guy to me for an interview" and "did they know he was going to show up dressed like he'd cobbled together an outfit from decade-old clothes left-over at the Salvation Army?"

Those thoughts combined over the next few minutes with a recognition of his penetrating eyes, his calmness, astuteness, and self-awareness that he wasn't the "typical" Italian candidate. I could "feel" there was something special about Carlo. It was something intangible that Carlo transmitted, told made me realize I should look past his attire and concentrate on the characteristics of the person.

Knowing that the importance of character traits trumps all else in determining success, I was curious to find out what it was about him that was special. I settled into the interview to discover—through broken communication—that he was very smart, intellectually curious, a quiet fighter with extreme competitiveness, unflappable, and courageous.

I constantly tried to throw him off balance, once telling him I didn't think he could do the job. He looked at me with a unique curiosity and sparkle in his eyes, "Really, why?" Essentially turning the question around on me. Instead of being defensive, I could see that he was genuinely curious. I could envision him asking himself, "Why does he think that?" At that moment, I realized Carlo wasn't here "to get a job"; he was here "to do a job."

I decided to hire Carlo. You could say I took a chance, but that's not how I saw it. I hired character. And character is the difference maker. Carlo Carpanelli wound up being the most successful sales rep in the world for the company, multiple years in a row, constantly sealing multi-million-dollar deals.

Andy asked, "I can see why character traits are critical, but are there specific characteristics you have found to be most important to the success of a rep?"

"There are a lot, but I'll narrow it down to my top five," I said. "Overall, you'll find that positive character traits are the key differentiators that separate those who continually excel from all the others."

These are my top five key positive characteristics:

Intelligence
PHD
Coachability and Adaptability
Integrity
Curiosity

CHARACTER TRAITS

INTELLIGENCE

A rep needs to have the intelligence to gain the knowledge required to succeed. An intelligent rep will quickly learn your product, competition, processes, methodologies, and customer persona use-case issues. And as companies grow, selling situations change due to new products, new services, new messaging, changing competition, and evolving customer pains. Every reps' knowledge needs to be constantly updated.

PERSISTENCE, HEART, AND DESIRE (PHD)

Skills are developed over time with incremental gains, through hundreds or thousands of iterations. They take a considerable amount of persistence and desire to master.

A national billiards Champion was once asked to explain the difference between winners and losers. He said, "The loser's practice until they get it right, and the winner's practice until they never get it wrong."

Persistence is paramount in skill development. It doesn't matter how intelligent someone is if they also don't possess the heart and desire to continually master new sales skills. As the sales process evolves, reps need to master new skills to execute new steps in the sales process.

COACHABILITY AND ADAPTABILITY

Multiple times, I've seen reps who are either too insecure to admit that they cannot perform a new function or too fearful of change. They won't let anyone coach them.

If you're not coachable, you won't learn.

If you won't learn, you won't adapt.

Adaptability is a critical trait in any rapidly growing company. As your product, market, competition, and company changes, you'll need people who are flexible enough to adapt to the changing environment. They'll need to perform new tasks, learn new products, and develop new skills.

I've also seen people who are coachable . . . but never adapt. They are willing to accept coaching, but, even after multiple coaching sessions, they still don't adapt. Is that a fear of change? Is it the courage to change? Is it a lack of drive to persist through change? Is it some deeper psychological issue?

I don't know. I *do* know that in fast-growing companies, people need to continually adapt. Lacking adaptability means that at some point in the growth of your company, your rep will be stuck in the past.

No dinosaurs needed.

INTEGRITY

According to the Oxford Language Dictionary, the definition of integrity is "*the quality of being honest and having strong moral principles, moral uprightness.*"

It's challenging to make the number every quarter without having to worry if everyone on your team is being honest and transacting deals with integrity.

You'll find that dishonest behavior, unethical dealings, or integrity issues quickly damage trust within the team. When trust is broken, the team struggles to build back a bond that, in many cases, can't be repaired.

CHARACTER IS THE DIFFERENCE MAKER

Character is such a difference maker that I've hired reps who had no sales experience, many reps who had no domain experience, and others who had no software-sales experience. When someone possesses the combination of high intelligence with off-the-chart competitiveness, adaptability, integrity and curiosity, find a way to hire them.

Overall, the most important thing to know about character traits is this:

If their mother and father couldn't change them by twenty years old, then you can't change them.

You won't be able to boost their I.Q., force them to be persistent, enhance their competitiveness, boost their adaptability, or expand their curiosity.

EXECUTION EXPERIENCE

"And by 'execution experience,' do you mean their track record, their resume?" asked Jim.

"Yes. The resume should only be a small part of the evidence of a candidate's fit to the position description."

"We've always based our entire decision on the resume. Why should it only be partial evidence of their abilities?" asked Andy.

First, the resume hasn't been certified by a third party.

Ever been to a website for a hotel, real estate property, or vacation destination in which the pictures and description highlight the possibility of a fantastic experience, which in reality is quite different?

That's because those sites were never verified for accuracy by a certified third party. A resume is no different. It's built by the candidate for the candidate. It's tailored to highlight the candidates' strengths and minimize or hide any deficiencies. It's your job to ask probing questions during the interview to discover the *reality*.

Second, the resume only reveals a track record of the positions and companies for which the candidate worked.

The descriptions typically don't reveal evidence of their specific knowledge, including, but not limited to, sales process, qualification methodology, or cost justifications. And it certainly won't disclose specific sales skills like perfection of cold calling, pipeline generation, presentation skills, objection handling, or listening and questioning skills.

Third, and most important, no resume unveils the candidate's core characteristics, including intelligence, drive, integrity, adaptability, and curiosity.

A resume is not a document to use as the basis for making a decision on a candidate. Base your decision on your customized *position description* with the specific knowledge, skills, characteristics, and experience required for success in your sales process and for your target accounts.

Jim said, "When we lose reps, no one seems to analyze why. As sales leaders, we have a habit of blaming the rep."

Jim had hit a good point. I explained, "If a sales leader loses a rep—who they hired—then that failure in on the leader. Not the rep. The leader needs to look in the mirror and hold themselves accountable."

1. Did I recruit the wrong person? If so, what did I miss in the interview process?
2. Is it because I couldn't develop the person due to my own lack of knowledge or skill in the same areas?
3. Is it because I can't lead my people? Do I not have an intimate knowledge of their strengths, weaknesses, motivations, and goals, which causes me to be unable to inspire them?

In all cases, the leader needs to accept responsibility, make changes, and adapt, or you'll make the same mistake again.

GETTING STARTED

"All this information is great, John," Jim said as he ran a hand through his hair. "But where do we start? How do we distill this information to our reps now?"

"Good sales managers get out from behind their desk to manage their businesses," I said. "Start there. Stop relying on the CRM system, email, and texting to manage your reps. Stop being a glorified scorekeeper managing your reps solely on KPI activities. Start understanding what's preventing them from successfully accomplishing each step in the sales process to advance deals. As you make calls with your reps, observe them. Observing is the only way for you to *intimately* understand the level of their skills and knowledge to help them sell and qualify accounts."

THE GOLF COACH

Many first-time managers give reps too many new skills to learn all at once. Since skills are developed over time, it's important to identify only one fundamental skill issue for them to develop at a time.

Think about a great golf coach. If you were taking lessons for the first time and the coach gave you five swing elements to develop at the same time, you'd find it difficult to master all of them simultaneously. If the coach kept telling you how you're doing it all wrong on every swing, you'd start to think that you are not meant to play the game of golf.

You'd think, "This person is the coach, and if the coach thinks I should be able to master all these swing elements at the same time, then this is not the game for me."

However, if the coach gave you one swing element. Told you how to grip the club and asked you to consistently hit the ball, that's something you could achieve.

Then, only after you could consistently hit the ball, the good coach gave you one more swing element. Asked you to keep your left arm straight during the swing and made you perform that element until you were consistent before giving you the next skill to develop. With continual practice, that's something you could master.

The coach is there to help through that never-ending process of:

Inspiring
Coaching and Developing
Inspecting

The coach would initially build your game from the perspective of basic skills and inspire your confidence at the same time. Become intimate with your reps' sales capabilities. Then, coach them on one skill until they have incorporated that skill into their DNA before moving to the next skill.

28
WITH THE SALES REPS

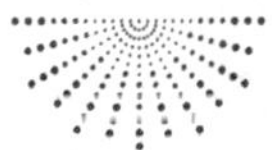

Weeks later, the quarter had ended.

I couldn't wait to see what was happening over at Forego. When I reached out to Raj to get an update on the quarter, I heard a glimmer of hope in his voice.

"You caught me in my office with Dennis. We had a much better quarter even though we didn't hit our plan number. We didn't have as many transactions, but the average deal size for new accounts has ticked up, and we sold a few larger deals. It's possible that those are early indicators that the team is learning how to qualify opportunities and sell differently."

"Our POV win rate was thirty-five percent this quarter, which reinforces that," added Dennis.

"Have you been on any calls with your team?" I asked.

"Once with Shannon and once with Kathleen, yes," said Dennis. "They are doing a better job of understanding and quantifying customer pains, but the team hasn't created a template from which reps can easily build a cost justification proving value.

Because of that, they're struggling to quantify pain. Even though they're trying, we aren't consistently getting high enough in accounts, and some reps are still prematurely pushing for a POV."

"From what I've seen, our ability to quantifying and implicate pain is not in our DNA yet," Raj noted. He went on to say that Andy's team almost made their quarterly number and had additional positive signs. The number of new logos increased on his team. The average deal size on his team moved from $50,000 to $55,000.

"Also, Andy seems better," Raj reported. "He's less frustrated. I see more teamwork and skill than brute force. We believe his team has made progress."

Jim's team also came close to their goal with the most new logos of any team. His average deal size climbed to almost $60,000.

"Jim's leadership shows as people are rallying around him," Raj said. "He will go places."

"Then would you mind if I made a sales call with a couple of reps? I want to see this in action before our next meeting. Watching the sales reps will help me understand what the managers have implemented. Then we'll know what to stress next time."

"Of course," Raj said. "We will set it up."

CALLS WITH HANNLIN AND SHANNON

Less than a week later, I hopped on the unfriendly skies of United and landed at George Bush International Airport in Houston. Hannlin met me there, ready to go, with not a stitch of clothing out of place as he sat outside baggage claim in a new BMW 5 Series.

Ten minutes later, Hannlin flew down Highway 59 at seventy-five miles per hour. A sales meeting at a global foodservice company in Houston named Sysco awaited us, and I was eager to see Hannlin in action on his sales calls. He'd been active in the discussions regarding Discovery and Scoping, so it would be interesting to see him put it to work.

"My goal is to get promoted to manager," Hannlin said while looking right at me. "Think the new sales process will help me do that?"

"Keep your eyes on the road, Hannlin. It's why you have ears on the side of your head. I'd like us to arrive safely."

He laughed. "So, coach, tell me what it's like to be a sales manager. Is it that different than being a rep?"

"Do you have any kids?" I asked.

"Yeah, two. Why?"

"Would you want to have five more kids?"

He turned to me with a puzzled expression.

"The road, Hannlin. Eyes on the road," I insisted. "Think of being a sales manager like this: when you were single, you only cared about yourself. You never worried about when you woke up, when you went to bed, what you ate, when you ate, or when you scheduled specific activities during the week and weekend. Right?"

A wistful expression came to his face. "Right. *Those* were the days."

"Being single is like being a sales rep," I continued as an exit flashed past us. "You only worry about yourself and making your number. Your calendar has your events, you only care about your pipeline, your accounts, your forecast, and the resources that help you make your quarterly number. It's all about you."

Understanding started to dawn on his face. His mouth rounded into an *O*, and I knew he was listening.

"Once you had children, your world changed. It wasn't about you anymore. Your world was now centered around your kids. When do they go to school? When are their sporting events? When do they need to eat and sleep? What do they need me to provide for them so they can be successful?"

His emphatic nod confirmed it. "I love my kids; you're right."

"I'll bet you love them! I'm also sure you have an intimate understanding of their strengths and weaknesses, right?"

At this, he gave a little nod. "Yeah, absolutely. My kids are different. They grow at different rates, have different interests and experience things differently."

"Exactly. All your kids have different strengths, weaknesses, and characteristics. You are doing everything to make them successful, right?"

"You bet."

I leaned back in the seat. "It's the same when you move from sales rep to sales manager. It's not about you anymore. Good sales leaders realize that it's about putting their people first. It's all about their reps. Gaining an intimate understanding of their reps' strengths, weaknesses, fears, desires, and motivations. It's the leader's job to find a way to make them successful."

"Ah," he said. "I never thought of it that way."

We arrived at the Sysco parking lot a few minutes later. He drew in a deep breath before we climbed out and headed inside for his first meeting with the CIO. Thankfully, he had done his homework.

"I read through the Sysco annual report, the Business Risks section of their 10-K, and Googled the CEO and CIO," he said. "I found some initiatives that the CEO said were imperatives for the current year, and the CIO, a person named Jess Stats, spoke of those challenges on a speaker panel. I know that Forego can help them with one of those initiatives."

"Then let's figure out what he has to say," I said, with the hope that Hannlin would find a potential Champion here.

Jess Stats, the CIO, had been with Sysco for seven years. Prior to that, he'd been with another major Houston food company named Kroger. Throughout the meeting, Hannlin was effective with specific, probing discovery questions, all of which were based on his diligent homework. Jess Stats made it clear he appreciated Hannlin's grasp on their business issue.

Hannlin had researched their environment and received confirmation from Jesse that Sysco needed a single tool for app build-time to run-time threat detection. They also needed cloud compliance for workloads, containers, and Kubernetes across Amazon-AWS, Microsoft-Azure, and Google GPS.

"We have another Houston customer, which I understand you may be familiar with—Kroger—that had the same issue as they released apps to multiple cloud environments," Hannlin said with confidence. "We've successfully remedied their security vulnerabilities and compliance issues with automated monitoring from a single platform. They have significantly driven down costs by freeing themselves from the burdens of unnecessary hardware, rule writing, and inaccurate alerts."

"I'm impressed with your command of this issue," Jesse said as he leaned back in his chair. "Who else in the company have you spoken with?"

"So far, no one else. I've just done my homework on your company," said Hannlin.

"That's even more impressive. How would you recommend we explore a partnership together?"

I mentally held my breath. An eager rep would dive into the partnership offer, but a wise one would get more information.

Hannlin smiled. "Of course, we're very interested in partnering with you, but do you mind if I ask a few more questions?"

"Sure."

"Who are you and the CEO holding personally responsible for heading the initiative?"

"Two people—Greg Workload, the VP of DevSecOps, and John Risk, the CISO."

"Who else in the company is involved in this decision?"

"A few development managers in Greg's organization and security leaders in John Flynn's organization. Someone they all listen to is a person named Joel Rodriquez."

"Can I tell Greg, John, and Joel that I have spoken with you?"

"Yes, of course."

"Have you been working with any other vendors?"

"Not yet. But a few other large vendors are always roaming the halls."

"Have any specific product capabilities been specified?"

"Yes. At the highest level, we're looking for a single platform that can handle security, compliance, and visibility across the Amazon, Microsoft, and Google cloud platforms."

"Is there a definitive timeframe for implementing a solution?"

"Great question. I can't go into detail, so let's say we're always worried about host vulnerabilities and container intrusions. In addition, we have a major audit in December. That leaves us less then ninety days to find and implement a solution."

"Has this project been budgeted, and who controls the budget?"

"Yes, it's budgeted, and I control the budget."

"After speaking with Greg, John, and Joel, would you mind if I share a high-level summary of my findings with you to understand if it aligns with your corporate strategy?"

"Of course not; I'd appreciate knowing what you uncover."

"And after my summary of findings, would you be willing to connect with the people at Kroger to understand what they have found?"

"No doubt."

After we left Sysco, Hannlin had a list of items to quickly complete: meeting with Greg, John, and Joel; deeply understanding the business issues from their standpoint; hopefully building Greg and John (but certainly Joel) into Champions; locking down a bullet-proof criteria and building a cost justification.

When we returned to his car, he let out a long exhale, then looked at me with a questioning gaze.

"So?" he asked. "How do you think that went?"

"Hannlin, I have to say that you were very impressive. Because you did your research on the buyer and investigated their pain, you controlled the meeting. The depth of your questions told him your grasp of the subject. Because of that, he gave you what you asked for: a high-level overview of the people, the problem, the priority, the budget, and the timeframe. Is there anything you may have missed?"

"Yes, I forgot to ask about the negative consequences to their business."

"That's right. You didn't uncover the entirety of the impact to their business, but don't beat yourself up. You found out about their current or potential vulnerability and an upcoming audit. In your next meetings, I suggest you collect more specific info from Greg, John, and Joel on the pains in their current process and why they believe they are vulnerable. Overall, you did a really good job. Just remember to dig deeper during your next meetings."

"I'll also need to earn the trust of Greg, John and Joel and see if one of them could be my champion."

"Perfect"

After calls on Sysco and Waste Management, Hannlin dropped me back at Bush International for my flight to Atlanta to make sales calls with Shannon.

Shannon and I made calls with her manager on Center Ice, Hattrick, and Blueline. I was surprised by Shannon's ability to be inquisitive during sales calls. She had a style that allowed her to ask very direct questions without making people feel offended.

She hadn't performed the level of homework that Hannlin had prior to entering her accounts, and it showed. During the meetings, she probed for mission-critical issues, but, with limited time, it was difficult for her to both search for and land on a pain without a specific target subject.

After the sales calls, we all hopped into an Uber. I was disappointed by Shannon's manager because after every sales call, he never debriefed the call and agreed on the next steps with Shannon. Frustrated when we entered an Uber for the third time, I asked both of them to put their mobile phones away for a few minutes and analyze what happened in the meeting, what went right, what went wrong and what is the next logical step.

What could possibly be more important after a sales call than to immediately debrief?

All in all, I had seen tremendous growth. Next quarter would come quickly, which was when we'd dive back into the rest of the sales process.

29

FINDING CHAMPIONS

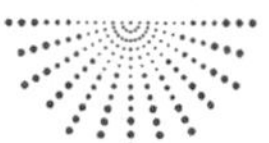

A week later, I took the 6:19 a.m. Acela Express into Penn Station and walked the seventeen blocks up to Fifty-First and Broadway. The conference room at Forego awaited. This would be a half-day session to check in after our first meeting, because I was going to meet them at their sales kickoff event in Las Vegas later in the month.

The group milieu had settled, and the sales managers seemed ready for me this time. No apprehension about what to expect, and an eagerness for me to tell them more. As soon as I was ready to dive in, Andy initiated the session with a question.

"We need help finding Champions," he said. "Since our last meeting, it's been obvious that we primarily end up with coaches, not Champions. Can you help us understand Champions and how we can find them?"

"OK, let's start with a company organization chart," I said. "What will an org chart tell us?"

ORG CHART VERSUS POWER CHART

"An org chart shows the hierarchy of the organization," Andy said, "the reporting structure through different departments, and the people in positional authority."

"That's right, Andy, positional authority, meaning people in managerial, directorial and vice-presidential roles. But what won't an org chart tell you?" I asked.

Jim raised his hand. "It won't tell you who has the influence to sway key decisions with either political connections, the capacity to guide, or the ability to control or alter decisions."

"In other words, just because someone has positional authority in a company, may not mean they have access to the Economic Buyer" I added.

I pitched a dry-erase marker to Jim and stepped back. "Build a 2x2 matrix on the board. Put INFLUENCE on the *x*-axis and AUTHORITY on the *y*-axis. This will help us display the four types of people in a company."

I took a picture of Jim's matrix:

Authority ⟶		
	Authority/No influence (ANI)	Influence + Authority (IA)
	No Influence/No Authority (NINA)	Influence/No Authority (INA)
	Influence ⟶	

The first step in finding your Champion is to uncover the *power chart* in an organization.

A power chart is similar to an org chart, but it specifically defines the influential people in the organization. The people with access to the Economic Buyer. We want to seek people with influence to become our Champions.

People on the power chart can reside at any level of the org chart, because true influence is independent of hierarchical standing.

Typically, but not always, people who have influence *and* authority (IA) have power though both their position in the company and their business acumen. These people could be your *business Champion.*

And people with influence but no authority (INA) are typically people with a deep domain expertise. These people could be your *technical Champion.*

Many times, the business Champion will seek the advice of a technical Champion to thoroughly evaluate a technical solution.

When it comes to buying for the company, an Economic Buyer consults with these people (IA's and INA's) to validate a new solution to a significant business issue. The Champion's expertise and credibility on past decisions has developed a reputation and allowed them to maintain influence within the company. Their influence gives them access to the Economic Buyer on future decisions.

Spending time with the NINAs and ANIs of the organization is not a total waste of time because you may find a coach. A coach may meet with you, understand the value of your product, give you inside information, want you to win, and coach you. Just don't expect that an NINA or ANI will ever have the influence or power, within the organization, to be your Champion.

"Then where are the best places to find Champions in a company?" Andy asked.

"Great question. Why don't we all brainstorm this? Andy, can you scribe?"

- Who is working on critical projects?
- Who was recently promoted?
- Who has been assigned to complete new initiatives?
- Who is held personally accountable for key company decisions?
- Who made the last major departmental purchase for the company?
- Who do the C-level executives confer with on critical company decisions?
- When presenting to a group at the company, whose statements are most influential?
- Who in group meetings asks very perceptive and deep-probing questions?
- Who do people say is most influential in these types of decisions?

In large accounts, every C-level executive typically has a number of operations people assigned to help them. It's a great place to seek information on potential Champions.

For instance, the CRO at a large company may have a VP Sales Ops, VP Sales Enablement, Sales HR, Sales Marketing, and Sales Finance Ops. Ops people usually know the major issues that the C-Level person struggles to solve, and they almost certainly know who influences the C-level in those decisions.

IT'S TOUGH TO FIND CHAMPIONS

"Carlos," I called. "Tell the group about our experience with Fujitsu when we made some sales calls together."

With a bright smile, he said, "I think it's best if you tell the story."

Carlos and I had just finished making several sales calls on Fujitsu Services in Irvine, California. After our final meeting, we headed toward the elevators, silently. We didn't speak as we left the elevator and crossed the lobby, and we were careful not to say any of our thoughts about our calls while inside the Fujitsu building.

As we moved through the parking lot, Carlos asked me, "What did you think about our sales calls?"

The calls had gone well, and we'd garnered new information, but the account wasn't progressing toward a forecastable deal. Multiple people had confirmed their known pain and their need to remedy the situation. We met with directors and VPs, who had established the negative repercussions of the problem on a key corporate business measure. Something obvious was lacking, and, without it, the deal wouldn't happen.

"I think we gained a lot of pertinent information for a deal, but we're missing a Champion. All the people we met had authority, but none of them are going to get us a meeting with the Economic Buyer. It's my sense that none of those people have real influence in the company."

"John, I get it. But it's been really difficult to find a Champion in Fujitsu. I've been calling on them for four months. I've looked high and low in the company, and I don't think there *is* a Champion."

"Absence of evidence is not evidence of absence," I said. "Just because you haven't seen an alien doesn't mean they don't exist. Just because you haven't found a Champion doesn't mean there isn't one."

I stopped walking, and Carlos followed suit. "Turn around and look at the building," I said.

We stared at the building with the Fujitsu logo in plain sight. The day had a gentle breeze that felt good after being inside for hours.

"Do you think there could be anyone in that building who could Champion us? Could there possibly be someone who cares about solving mission-critical business pain with a compelling business outcome? Someone with the power to help us access the Economic Buyer?"

Carlos looked at me, let out a long breath, then quietly turned to toward his car. We walked in silence and hopped into his car. Carlos pressed the ignition button, turned to me and said, "There's got to be a Champion in there."

Weeks later, Carlos called me to tell me he'd identified a Champion during a presentation to multiple people at Fujitsu. One person was asking probing questions about both the technology and the business results of implementing the technology at other companies.

Sensing that this person had all the characteristics of a potential Champion, Carlos arranged a one-on-one meeting with the person. After a scoping session, this person helped Carlos build the start of a powerful cost justification. At the same time, Carlos confirmed that the person had influence in the account by checking with people at different levels of Fujitsu. Ultimately, the person became Carlos's Champion and partnered with Carlos on a large opportunity.

30
WHY WOULD SOMEONE BE YOUR CHAMPION?

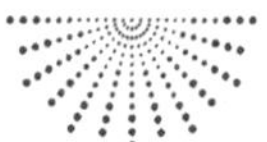

"Carlo's story illustrates a great point about why we have to discover a Champion," Jim said, hand half-raised. "What I don't fully understand is why would any person want to be a Champion?"

"Champions have personal aspirations," I said. "To realize those aspirations, they need to differentiate themselves within the organization. One way to do that is to solve notable business problems. It's a way for them to obtain a personal win by being recognized for their efforts and showing their added value to the company.

If your product is a solution to a crucial business problem, that *directly effects one of the champion's job measures or a major company measure*, it could give them what they desire: a personal win. Think of the person with a sign on their forehead that reads, "What's in it for me?". We have to answer that question when selling to a potential Champion."

Personal wins could be as simple as the following:

- **Recognition**: Being recognized as a company problem solver, productivity enhancer, or cost cutter
- **Control**: Gaining control over the implemented solution and all the users of the solution
- **Productivity**: Increasing the productivity of their entire department
- **Promotion**: Obtaining a promotion in recognition for their continued problem-solving efforts
- **Status**: Gaining status by tying their name to a business solution

31
EARNING TRUST

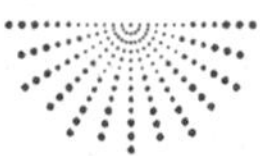

"So, John," Andy said. "Sometimes my reps swear they found an IA or an INA that could be a potential Champion, but after the person hears our sales pitch, they're reluctant to be our Champion. What could cause that?"

"'You have to earn their trust."

Champions are intellectually astute and politically shrewd. They're careful in two predominant ways:

Will not align to small pains
Won't attach to unprepared salespeople

Champions won't jeopardize their standing in the company or their influence and reputation with the Economic Buyer over a salesperson who doesn't understand their business. Or one who is incapable of articulating, in business terms, how they can solve a serious business problem.

Reps need to understand that the reputation of the Champion is at stake. The Champion wants to work with a trusted business partner to ensure the solution will be successful or their reputation will be tarnished.

Andy stared at me a bit startled.

I laid it out this way, "Let's say your rep found major pain in the company. You're probably thinking, *my rep found pain and pain finds Champions*. But there's more to it than finding pain. Your rep is just another salesperson until they have *differentiated themselves as a trusted business partner* through excellence during Discovery and Scoping. Your rep needs to prove they're a rep with integrity and can be trusted."

When any rep enters a sales opportunity, they have to overcome the natural objections people have which are:

No pain
No urgency
No money
No trust

Your rep found a major pain, your rep implicated pain to drive urgency but now your rep needs to earn the trust of a Champion that has access to the Economic Buyer, who has control of the budget.

Once a sales rep *finds* a potential Champion, they have to *earn that person's trust*. Reps will only be capable of building trust when they selflessly live in the customer's shoes. They must have the Champion's best interest in mind, which is achieved by viewing the situation from the customer's vantage point.

Good Champion-builders aren't selfish. They're selfless.

They are authentic and curious like Carlo.

No gimmicks.

SELFLESS STORY

I think this is best illustrated in a short story.

A very old, wise man told a young salesperson to go to the window and look outside.

So, the young salesperson did.

"What do you see?" asked the wise man.

"I see a number of potential customers."

"Now, go over to the mirror. Tell me what you see."

"I see myself, of course."

"Why is that? Both the window and the mirror are made of glass."

"Because the mirror has a backing of silver, which makes me see myself."

"Exactly," said the wise man. "When salespeople let silver get between themselves and their customers, they no longer have a clear view of their customers. They only think of themselves."

Earn trust.

Be selfless.

DEVELOPING TRUST

"Is there a method you use to help develop trust?" asked Kathleen.

"In simple terms, I don't act like I'm interested, I am genuinely interested in the customer's issues. I ask a lot of questions, listen intently and constantly confirm my understanding of the personal and company situation with the customer. Trust is developed over time through a simple, *never-ending process* of Asking, Messaging, and Confirming with customers to understand their issues and align to their expectations."

The process can be broken into simple steps:

1. Asking:
Prepared Discovery and Scoping questions

2. Messaging:
Alignment of the potential solution to the pain and company fit

3. Confirming:
Agreement of the message or realigning of the message by asking

HOW CHAMPIONS EVALUATE TRUST

"That's simple enough. How do you think a Champion evaluates trust?" Jim asked.

A Champion *evaluates trust through their expectations of value. There are three value elements Champions evaluate:*

Business Value of the Solution
Do they trust that the solution completely solves their business problem?
Do they trust that the future gain far outweighs the current pain in an ROI?
Do they trust that the solution will drive measurable impact on business goals?

Performance Value of the Company

Do they trust that the company will perform to support the Champion and product throughout an implementation?
Do they trust that the company will perform in helping to *adopt* the solution with their people?
Do they trust that the company will perform in helping to *optimize* the product in their environment?

Experience Value of the Salesperson
Has the experience of dealing with the salesperson developed a quality of trust?
Has the experience of working with the salesperson demonstrated that they will be an ally to manage a successful implementation?
Has the overall experience of working with the salesperson developed into a business partnership?

32
EDUCATING THE CHAMPION

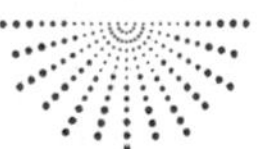

Educate your Champion on relevant issues. If you don't, you'll lose them later in the sales process. You want to ensure they don't get caught flat-footed on known product limitations, competitive traps, or implementation impediments.

Educate them on everything from the competition's product, competitive traps, and common objections. Show them how to justify your product internally. Have them speak to Champions in your installed base. Arrange meetings for them with executives at your company. All of this is done in the vein of educating a Champion, not selling.

Once you believe you have a potential Champion, selling ceases to be selling.

Selling becomes educating.

"You'll also need to educate your Champion to be an internal sales rep," I told the room, but looked at Andy. Jim had this sort of relationship in hand, but Andy focused on more direct measures. This would be particularly important for him.

Jim lifted a hand. "Kathleen and I experienced the positive results of investing in the education a Champion recently," he said.

I motioned for Jim to share.

"Kathleen forecasted a half-million-dollar deal with UPS, which had me worried. In fact, both of us were uneasy, because we weren't sure we had done everything possible to educate her Champion at UPS," Jim said, "and we were naturally paranoid since it was a half-million-dollar deal.

"The day before the Champion was to meet with the Economic Buyer, Kathleen secured a new meeting with the Champion.

"'Can we role play your meeting with the Economic Buyer?' she asked.

"The Champion looked at us and told us not to worry, but Kathleen responded, 'Well, I *am* worried. Together you and I have done a lot of work. We've reviewed everything from your business pain, the cost justification, and your desired business outcome. We've even discussed objections the Economic Buyer will be sure to ask. We need this meeting to be successful.'"

At that moment, the Champion surprised both of them by showing his prepared notes on everything the Economic Buyer could possibly ask. All the potential objections, the competition, the cost justification, and quantified business outcome.

"The Champion's answers made us feel secure that Kathleen had fully prepared the Champion for the Economic Buyer meeting," Jim said.

A few weeks later, Kathleen secured the deal for a little over one million dollars.

Kathleen had done an excellent job in educating the Champion prior to the meeting, but, in that meeting, she also tested him and verified that she had a real Champion.

33
TESTING THE CHAMPION

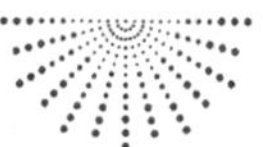

"After you have done a thorough discovery investigation *and have earned the trust* of a potential Champion through the Scoping process, why is it important to test your Champion?"

Andy said, "Because today, we just hope that the person giving us information is our Champion, but usually we find out too late that they're just a good coach."

"Right, so how could we test to see if they are a coach or a Champion?"

"We can ask different levels of questions to test their knowledge," said Jim.

"OK, let's write some of those down."

QUESTIONS TO TEST CHAMPIONS

- How are items purchased at XYZ company?
- What is the typical evaluation process for new products?
- Who made the last few major purchases?

- Can they help you map out the *as-is* process?
- Can they detail why the identified company pain could be classified as "major"?
- Can they explain the implications of not solving the pain?
- How do they see that your solution provides business value?
- How does the competition's solution provide business value?
- Can they tell you what happened during the meeting with the competition?

WHAT ACTIVITIES COULD WE ASK THEM TO PERFORM?

- Arrange a demonstration to a different department
- Facilitate an introduction to another stakeholder in the decision process
- Share any product evaluation documents
- Call a customer reference
- Sponsor a meeting with the Economic Buyer
- Help you create the POV criteria
- Introduce you to the Legal and Procurement contacts
- Help you craft a cost justification

Warning: *Testing a Champion should only be done at the right time.*

Many tests of a potential Champion may be premature if you haven't performed your due diligence on their environment and found the "pain above the noise." And if you haven't earned their trust and educated them on everything from how your product solves their business issues to the competitions' product and your cost justification, you aren't ready to ask these things of them.

Too many salespeople "burn" a potential Champion by prematurely asking them to do something before they've proved to the potential Champion that they performed their own due diligence and have earned the trust of Champion.

Don't be selfish.

TESTING A QUALIFIED CHAMPION

"Can I tell a story about a meeting where we tested the limits of a Champion to get the Economic Buyer?" Andy asked. "It really shows the way we interacted with and tested a Champion."

I motioned for him to go next. Andy took the floor.

"One of my sales reps, Paul, had a sizable deal on the forecast from a large insurance company named Northwest Insurance in the Midwest. He had a $500,000 deal in his forecast's 'most likely' section and another $500,000 in the 'best-case' section. After asking a few questions, it became clear that he was being blocked by his Champion, a director.

"The director said he wanted to buy $500,000 of Forego software but refused us access to the CIO—who was the Economic Buyer. That seemed strange to me," Andy said. "Why would someone who had made sizable prior purchases with us say they wanted to make a $500,000 purchase but not allow us access to the Economic Buyer?"

Immediately, Andy started to wonder if Paul really controlled the deal or if he was being controlled. If the director was attempting to maintain control in order to broker a large discount or was playing the same controlling game with the competition, Paul could have lost the deal completely.

"Without access to the Economic Buyer, we simply didn't know if we were in control of the deal," Andy said. "What we did know from our Discovery process was that the organization required a purchase larger than $500,000 to achieve their stated business goals. I thought maybe the director really was Paul's Champion and did want to buy more than $500,000, because his signature authority was only $500,000, and he was afraid to go to the CIO to ask for more money."

Paul and Andy decided to roll the dice. They would win together or lose together. They wanted to truly qualify the deal by scheduling a meeting with the Economic Buyer. And, if there was a deal, go for the one-million-dollar price tag.

"It was a very uncomfortable situation for Paul and me," Andy admitted, "but trying new things like testing a Champion requires us to be comfortable with being uncomfortable."

So, they hatched a plan. They played good guy/bad guy. Unbeknownst to the director, Andy called the CIO and scheduled a meeting with him, which would start at the end of Paul's previously scheduled meeting with the director. The director thought he was meeting only with Paul.

"When we met with the director," Andy said, "we politely tried to persuade him to make the larger purchase for one million dollars. As we presented our offer, the director was fuming. He squirmed uncomfortably in his chair. Then he started to yell at us. He pointed his finger directly at Paul, and, in a raised voice said, 'I'm not interested in making a larger purchase! I've already rejected Paul's previous offers.'"

The yelling made Paul very nervous. Andy could see in Paul's eyes that Paul believed this was a terrible idea and that the chance of completely blowing up the deal was real.

Still, Andy pressed on.

"I tried to calm the director down. I told him that we were simply offering him a purchase option based on the Discovery and Scoping sessions Paul had with him and his team."

What they offered was reasonable and not out of the ordinary, based on the director's stated business needs.

"I was honest with the Director," Andy said. "I told him that I had instructed Paul to make the larger offer. Then, I informed him that I, without Paul knowing, had scheduled a meeting with the CIO."

The director simmered and glared at Andy.

Faced with the fact that they had already scheduled a meeting with the CIO, Andy started to sense mixed emotions from the director.

"He seemed . . . scared," Andy said. "He clearly didn't want to face the CIO and personally ask to make the larger purchase. On the other hand, he seemed relieved that *we* would be the 'bad guys' asking for the larger purchase. Even he could play good guy/bad guy with the CIO."

They walked into what seemed like an old-time '80s-style office with shag-carpeted floors, wooden walls, and a sprawling desk in front of draped windows. On his desk sat a wooden plaque facing out, ensuring that everyone recognized his title.

"I thanked the CIO and told him why we'd requested the meeting," Andy said. "I asked if he was familiar with our solution and if making a purchase was still a priority for him."

The CIO said it was a priority and informed them why he was committed to solving the business issue. It ended up being a cordial and professional discussion.

"I could sense the director, sitting to my right, become more nervous than a long-tailed cat in a room full of rocking chairs," Andy said with a laugh. "I told the CIO his director had done a professional job working with my team. That he'd allowed us to gain a deep understanding of the specific needs of their business environment. Given that solving his issues was a top priority, I presented him with the option of the larger purchase, incorporating all of their business drivers and outlining the impact a larger purchase would have on his company operations."

The CIO told Andy he believed the larger purchase would allow them to achieve their business goals in a faster timeframe. Then he looked at the director and said, "If you agree, we should proceed immediately."

The director shook his head in agreement.

"Once the meeting was over," Andy said, "I saw a different person in the director. He was obviously relieved and quite happy. As we ambled down the hallway, he displayed a different side of himself. He commended Paul for his hard work. He now had a green light to make the larger purchase—a purchase that made his life simpler."

"It shows that even our Champions have certain limits that need to be tested." Andy said.

TESTING STEALTH CHAMPIONS-THE PROFESSIONAL WALK AWAY

Another manager raised her hand. "Does a Champion also have to coach you?"

"No, a Champion may be a *fox* or *stealth Champion*. Sometimes for political or company policy issues, these people understand the business value of your solution and adeptly help shape the decision criteria and decision process without explicitly tying themselves to you or your solution."

Stealth Champions are usually situated at high levels of a company. I've seen organization leaders coach their people to refrain from displaying favoritism toward a rep during an RFP process. In one instance, a rep of mine named Scott was calling on a large pharmaceutical company, which had a committee-run RFP process.

Scott had been calling on the account for six months, gaining an intimate understanding of their pains, process, and the players, while educating the players on how our product solved their pains. So, he was naturally surprised to find that the POV criteria didn't include our key product differentiators.

Scott called to ask for advice on the situation. He was frustrated, after working with the committee for months and he hadn't identified a Champion. In addition, the POV criteria was not in our favor.

My advice to Scott was to professionally walk away from the account. He was initially shocked by my advice and obviously nervous to walk away from his six months of work in a major account. Naturally, he imagined negative repercussions. To Scott's credit, he composed a detailed and very respectful letter, stating his reasons for withdrawing for consideration of their business.

What would he have to lose? *Nothing*. If the company allowed him to walk, it meant he didn't have a stealth Champion, and they didn't see business value in his product offering. In this scenario, he would have wasted more of his time in a futile effort by staying.

If Scott had performed his job well and built trust with the committee, someone in the account would reach out to Scott and request that he not detach from the POV. Which is exactly what happened.

Within two hours of Scott sending his letter, several people on the committee called Scott and asked, "What are you doing? Why are you leaving?" They told Scott that they not only liked him but saw value in his product.

With his confidence boosted, Scott returned to the account and reeducated the committee on why they needed to add several of our specific capabilities to their POV criteria to solve their particular pains. If they refused, and that was their prerogative, Scott would need to respectfully disengage, since it would be clear that *they were not buying what he was selling*.

The committee made the changes, in writing, to the POV criteria, which made it clear that Scott had Champions and was poised to win the POV. And that was exactly what had happened. Scott won the POV and a multi-million-dollar deal.

More importantly, Scott had learned valuable lessons in building trust, educating customers on the benefits and value of his solution, setting decision criteria in his favor, and testing stealth Champions.

TESTING A CHAMPION-THE BOSS

"Are there other ways to test a potential Champion?" Andy asked.

Good guy/bad guy is a simple but effective test.

Everyone has a boss, so everyone can relate to the situation. You explain to your potential Champion that your boss thinks you've been spending too much time at the account. He believes there isn't a potential sale at the account and that you've been wasting your time because they'll never buy. Your boss thinks you should walk away.

You ask the customer, "Would you have any advice for me? What should I tell my boss?"

Their answer will tell you if you should stay or go.

34

HOW DO YOU KNOW YOU HAVE A CHAMPION?

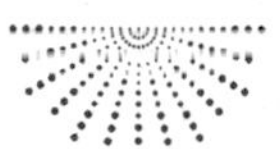

"Then how do you recognize that you have a Champion?" Jim asked. "You mentioned testing."

"Jim," I answered, "testing is just one method, but you'll know you have a Champion when you are in control. When items in the sales process turn from *unpredictable to predictable*."

For instance, in Scott's example, his sale was completely unpredictable prior to testing his stealth Champions. After testing, the company changed the criteria, and his sale status moved to predictable. Scott's key differentiators had been incorporated into the criteria by his Champions, allowing him to predict winning the account.

Since Champions help you stay in control, the remaining steps in the sales process are predictable. You should never be surprised. The account events occur exactly as you discussed with your Champion.

Predictable.

In control.

In other cases, *Champions are collaborative.* You *collaborate* together on the critical components of the sale. Critical sales process information flows between you and your Champion. Together, you create the decision criteria with your differentiators and formulate the steps of the decision process. It's a collaborative information exchange.

Through the collaboration, you should feel confident to *test your Champion's command of the deal.* Test their knowledge of the cost justification and articulation of the product's capability to solve their pain. You and your Champion are constantly trading information regarding account events. Their agenda is your agenda.

Collaborative.

In control.

And many times, this control is demonstrated through their actions. *They're proactive.* They are invested in openly introducing you to other key players in their company. They call to you discuss the competitions' presentation. They want to speak with your customer references. And they request discussions with your top company executives. Their actions tell you they have a vested interest in the success of the deal.

Proactive

In control.

35
DIFFERENCE BETWEEN A COACH AND A CHAMPION

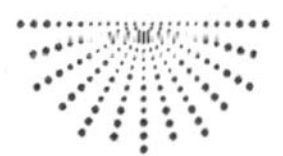

Jim said, "Many of our reps have a tendency to hang onto coaches throughout an entire sales process with the hope that they could somehow become a Champion. They're blind to the fact that a competitor has identified a real Champion. They waste all their time and company resources on a nice friendship with a coach, but the competition wins because they have a Champion."

"That's right Jim," I said. "The number one mistake most salespeople make is confusing a coach with a Champion."

A NINA or ANI may be a coach, a recommender, a technical buyer, a gate keeper, but they will never be a Champion. Even though the coach may give you information, introduce you to other people, and have a vested personal interest in your winning the business, but without influence or access to power, they will never be your Champion.

"Then what Champion indicator do you look for when you make sales calls with reps?" Jim asked.

When first introduced, I listen carefully to the person's view on the world. Typically, a coach looks through what I call *small eyes of product fit*. They understand how your product can solve what may be a big problem for them, but it's a small problem for the business.

They speak in *technical terms* and ask detailed technical questions. They never link the problem to a business solution with measurable impact on a major company measure.

Champions look through the *large eyes of business fit*. The lens of large business problems. Remember the firefighter *vs*. forest ranger story? They address those issues *above the noise*. They need to understand how your technology translates to a business outcome.

They speak in *business terms* and ask business questions to solve substantial business problems.

This is the reason you need to speak in business terms to find a high-level Champion. If you only speak in technical product terms as you get higher in an organization, *you'll get relegated down the organization to the level you sound like.*

After working with someone for a period of time, I've found the following major difference between coaches and Champions:

Coaches provide information but *never take action*

Champions *take action*

Here are the differences between a coach and a Champion:

	Coach	Champion
Provides information about company and competition	X	X
Coaches you during the sale	X	X
Has an interest in your winning	X	X
Has influence in the company		X
Gives you access to people on the power chart		X
Gives you access to the Economic Buyer		X
Sells for you when you are not in the account		X
Has authority in the account	maybe	maybe
Will co-author the decision criteria		X
Will provide internal metrics for a cost justification		X
Will help control the decision process		X

A coach cannot also be a Champion, but a Champion could also be an effective coach. A coach can't be a Champion because they don't influence others or have access to the Economic Buyer. But a Champion could also be a coach because they could coach you and give you inside information.

36
ECONOMIC BUYERS NEED A CHAMPION

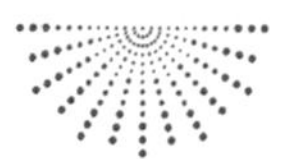

For political reasons, and, more importantly, implementation issues, Economic Buyers don't want to explicitly endorse your solution and be a visible Champion. The times I've seen the Economic Buyer as a stealth Champion, their power allowed them to adeptly nurture the decision criteria and guide the decision process to steer the decision in my company's favor.

Jim shared an experience in which his Champion was also the Economic Buyer. One of his reps, Shannon, was selling a deal to the CIO of T-Mobile. Shannon had had T-Mobile on her forecast for $500,000 for the last two quarters, but the deal had never closed. Yet, she forecasted the deal a third time.

Jim understood that he needed to confirm the priority for a purchase with the Economic Buyer or take the deal off the forecast. He arranged a meeting with the CIO at the RSA Conference at the Moscone Center in San Francisco.

The CIO agreed to meet Jim at a Starbucks across from the Moscone center. As they sat down, the CIO said, "I've only been in this job for eight months. I've used that time to set my priorities for the business. However, the former CIO had different priorities and started implementing an IT solution that used up all of my internal resources."

Once his team was finished implementing the last CIO's solutions, the current CIO committed to Jim to purchase Shannon's solution for $500,000.

"As a CIO, I can't implement the solution by myself," he explained. "I need someone under me, whom I can hold accountable for a successful implementation."

"The CIO told me he wanted the results contained in the cost justification to be realized so he could limit the risk of a poor implementation," said Jim.

Every salesperson needs a Champion to get a sale.

Every Economic Buyer needs a Champion to ensure they obtain the desired results after the implementation. It's why few Economic Buyers are your only Champion

WHY YOU NEED A CHAMPION FOR YOUR IMPLEMENTATION:

1. They can make the implementation successful.
2. They minimize any problems with your solution while you remedy the issue.
3. They can be a great customer reference.
4. Post implementation, they can help you quantify the business value of your solution for renewals and upsells.
5. They prevent the competition from attacking your installed account.
6. They prevent churn.

37
THE COMPETITION'S CHAMPION

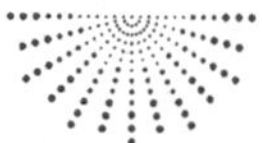

A sales leader should always consider whether or not the reps' Champion is stronger than the competition's Champion.

In an internal meeting, if the rep's Champion and the competitor's Champion get into a dispute, who will win?

With whom will people side with?

"So, whomever our Champion is," Jim said, "we need to ensure that we educate and prepare them as much as possible for traps and objections set by the competition."

"It would be even better if we find multiple Champions or Champions higher in the organization to counter the competitor's Champion," added Andy.

I pointed at Andy. "Exactly."

38
THE ECONOMIC BUYER

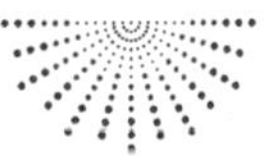

A month later, I joined Forego in Las Vegas at their annual sales kickoff, which included managers and reps worldwide. I flew into McCarron Airport, where people threw their last gambling dollars into slot machines, grabbed my bag, and headed for the long line of people waiting for a yellow taxi. Besides NYC, Vegas may be the only other city in which Uber and Lyft haven't killed the taxi yet.

The driver dropped me at the Encore Hotel entrance. After checking in—and a quick gym workout—I showered and headed for the meeting in a reserved conference room.

Since the checkup meeting, I'd had with the group, Raj requested that I make a few more sales calls with the reps and managers.

Carlos, Kathleen and Hannlin started to find Champions in many of their accounts, which made them feel more in control. In those accounts, they were able to get their product differentiators into the decision criteria, helping them win a few more POVs.

Shannon had discovered Champions in several accounts, who agreed to set a meeting with the Economic Buyer after learning more about her product, customers, competition, and business case.

"I'm ready for the next lesson, John!" Andy said. "I need to know everything I can about meeting with an Economic Buyer."

Which happened to be the third step in the Sales Process, and exactly what I planned to cover that day.

DEFINING THE ECONOMIC BUYER

"Let's switch gears. What do you think is the definition of an Economic Buyer?" I asked, dry-erase marker in hand.

A chorus of answers came from them.

"The person with the budget."

"The person who *approves* the budget."

"The finance person who approves the purchase."

"The CFO."

"In some ways, you're all close," I said. "But those answers are all completely different. Let's set a common definition we can all use."

The Economic Buyer (EB) is the person with discretionary use of the funds.

That means they have discretion over the budget, can reallocate budget from one project to another or from one allocated purchase request to another, and they have the authority to make the final decision. Only the EB can confirm whether or not buying your product is a priority.

With that as the definition, the Economic Buyer meeting becomes the *Go/No-Go stage of the sales process*.

THE ECONOMIC BUYER MEETING

Think of the Economic Buyer meeting as a wall.

When you have a successful EB meeting in which the customer's priority to buy and funds to make the purchase are confirmed, you've made it over the wall. You get to complete the remainder of the process.

An unsuccessful meeting means you hit a wall: your sales process is over.

"Why would our sales process be over?" asked Jim.

"Because the EB has discretion over the budget. Your product wasn't budgeted for, and the EB decided that your product wasn't a priority on which to reallocate budget."

I went on to explain that reps need to meet the EB prior to the POV, to frame and finalize the evaluation of their product differentiators against the decision criteria. That's why information-gathering and preparation *prior to* the Economic Buyer meeting is critical. Your ability to find a large business pain, develop trust with a Champion, and set the POV criteria will determine your success in the EB meeting and the sale. It's the critical reason reps need to slow down during Discovery and Scoping stage.

"Those EB meetings are daunting," Steve (we all called him Stevie Mac), a manager in from the UK said. "Economic Buyer meetings have me as nervous as a long-tailed cat in a room full of rocking chairs. I feel like I'll hit that wall you mentioned."

"Calm down when you're going in," I said. "It's normal to be a little anxious. In most sales processes, reps get nervous when meeting the Economic Buyer. However, if you've coordinated with your Champion and are prepared for the meeting, the majority of Economic Buyer meetings are confirmatory."

The key to a successful meeting is how you prepare for it with your Champion. You need to ensure that you have agreement on the EB meeting deliverables and the talk track with your Champion prior to the meeting. This preparation frames the topics, roles and especially the guardrails for the meeting, which will give your Champion comfort with the agenda and proposed outcome."

In the majority of cases, Champions will brief the Economic Buyer prior to the meeting, making the meeting ceremonial. In a typical EB meeting, you need to substantiate the following with the EB:

1. A high level summary of your Discovery and Scoping findings
2. The company's current state. The *as-is*
3. The negative consequences of that current state
4. Your proposed state. The *to-be*
5. The benefits of the future state
6. The required capabilities to achieve that future state
7. Customer success stories with quantified before/after metrics
8. Description of your solution based on the criteria
9. Confirmation of the remaining decision-process steps

Stevie Mac nodded as he thought that over.

"There are a few things you can do that may help ease your nerves," I continued with the steps I'll share here.

First, do your homework.

Eight of ten executives say that sales meetings are a waste of their time because salespeople are unprepared. You can't walk into the office of an Economic Buyer and hammer them with

Discovery and Scoping questions! They don't have the time or patience to help you do your job. You need to have done your homework before you enter their office. Doing your homework will make you less nervous.

Second, be a business partner.

Be someone who helps them run their business. Don't explain business issues they already know. Instead, inform them about a *business* issue they didn't consider. Explain the things they haven't thought of that directly affect what their business could be doing.

Research the company website, annual reports, 10-K report, shareholder letters, and analyst presentations to understand the customer better. It will help you have confidence.

Third, position your solution to align with the company's and their job performance measures.

For instance, link your solution to affect the company's revenues, costs, and risks at the corporate level and their personal job measures like time to market, employee productivity and application quality. This will spur interest and pertinent questions from the EB, giving you confidence, your solution is resonating.

Fourth, speak to the Economic Buyer on *their* business terms.

The terms that resonated with your Champion may or may not be the same terms that resonate with the Economic Buyer. The typical Economic Buyer is on the executive team or reports to the executive team and may have a slightly different view of the world than your Champion.

Fingers tapping their laptops could be heard as they took notes.

A BIG LENS

Let me tell you a story of a very memorable EB meeting which is an example of an EB agenda but also highlights the difference between the lens a Champion and the lens of an EB.

I worked with a first-line manager in Sweden named Goran.

I made numerous sales calls with Goran and his team, trying to sell our CAD (Computer Aided Design) software to ABB Transformers in Vasteras, Sweden.

When we started the sales process, we thought a man named William was the Economic Buyer because he was the VP Worldwide Engineering for ABB Transformers. Through the Discovery and Scoping process, we'd uncovered major pains with significant effects on their potential business outcome. Goran and his rep, Glenn, had done an incredible job of finding and educating William on the power of our software. Together, they had built a detailed business case to justify a thirty-million-dollar deal.

By the end of the Scoping process, the size and sphere of the cost justification changed the account dynamic so that William went from being an EB to being our Champion to help secure funding for the proposed project.

He arranged for Goran and I to meet with his boss, the VP Worldwide Production, at their corporate headquarters in Zürich, Switzerland.

As we entered the office of the corporate Economic Buyer and sat in the front of his large desk, I remember looking at Goran. I sensed a bit of nervousness. In his eyes, lingered a conflict between confidence and doubt. Confidence that he'd done a good job but . . . doubt that he'd performed everything necessary to secure a large deal.

Then the meeting started.

At a very high level, we summarized the details to justify the purchase, which was no different than any other meeting with an Economic Buyer. Then we launched into a typical high-level agenda for an Economic Buyer meeting.

1. **As-is vs. To-be:** Goran discussed their current *as-is* process versus the proposed *to-be* process for designing transformers.
2. **Pain-Discovery Statement:** Goran explained how, with William (our Champion) and his team, we discovered the current business pains.
3. **Quantified-Pain Statement:** We understood that it took twenty-six weeks, cost *X*-amount of dollars, and took *Y*-amount of people to design a transformer. ABB's time to market on transformer projects had been increasing, which, in turn, increased product costs by $*X*-million due to lost engineering productivity. That delayed time to market by *X*-weeks and potentially lost *Y*-percent of the market share to the competition.
4. **Implications of Not Solving the Pain:** If the issue wasn't resolved, the business would require additional highly paid engineers to decrease time to market but would increase costs and make ABB less price competitive.
5. **Business Outcome Statement:** Solving these issues would create a positive business outcome. An engineering productivity increase of *X*-percent would drastically reduce costs by $*X*-million and decrease time to market by *X*-number of weeks. That would allow ABB to be more price competitive and gain estimated market share of *Y*-percent in the global-transformer market.

6. **Required Capabilities and Differentiators:** After careful diligence with William and his team—and based upon interactions with our customers who'd had similar issues—we believed a solution to solve these issues would need to contain the minimum required capabilities. (Here we outlined our unique and comparable differentiators, which aligned to their specific pains).
7. **Decision Criteria for the Validation Event:** Therefore, we had incorporated those required capabilities into the decision criteria to validate our solution capabilities. (Here we listed our unique differentiators).
8. **Preliminary ROI:** Based upon ABB's internal cost numbers, we believed that ABB would be able to achieve a return on an investment (ROI) of 30.6 million dollars. We were quite confident of the ROI, since many of our customers had had very similar issues.
9. **Customer Success Stories:** As an example of a company with similar issues, ABC corporation, prior to using our solution, had the same issues in trying to increase engineering productivity and decrease time to market. After implementing our solution, ABC corporation decreased time to market by twenty percent and reduced engineering costs by $*X*-million.

After we finished, the Economic Buyer looked directly at Goran and me, complimented us on a professional presentation, and then said, "I see things differently than you see them."

Differently?

His statement rocked us.

I glanced at Goran. He sat stone faced, even though I could tell he was feeling sick.

Naturally, we both thought his statement was the beginning of the end.

I asked him, "What do you mean, differently?"

"Your cost justification is detailed and absolutely one way of cost justifying a 30.6 million dollar spend. But let me tell you why I view things differently. We build transformers in ten different facilities around the world. In those facilities, we generate twenty percent scrap. Yes, twenty percent of what we produce goes to the scrap yard. That scrap cost is equivalent to having two of our ten plants not working. So, it's not just engineering productivity that helps justify the purchase.

"Prior to this meeting, William shared with me how the accuracy of your drawings for manufacturing will reduce production scrap by twenty percent. If you can prove the accuracy of drawings in the POV, it will allow me to essentially recapture the production of two plants, which easily justifies your 30.6-million-dollar request."

This story was a fantastic lesson on how quickly a high-level Economic Buyer can cost-justify a business solution. They do it through the big-picture lens of their entire business.

The higher up you go, *the bigger the picture, the larger the lens.*

Our Champion looked at the issue through the big eyes of *worldwide engineering productivity*, which would lower product engineering costs and speed time to market, but the corporate Economic Buyer stared through a larger lens of enhancing *worldwide production*, which would decrease production costs, expand transformer production and, in turn, improve the potential number of transformers sold.

"You guys had a powerful Champion, because he probably knew he could justify the spend just through your engineering-productivity cost justification and could appeal to his boss on production scrap," said Hannlin.

"You also thought William was the EB because of his VP Worldwide Engineering title, but you must have been surprised that he was also your Champion?" asked Andy.

"Yes and no. It was tricky. We knew he was our Champion and EB for worldwide engineering productivity, but he was also the Champion we needed to gain approval from the EB for ABB Transformers worldwide. In the end, William, achieved multiple personal wins. He could increase productivity and decrease costs in his engineering operations and won the favor of his EB by helping the EB reduce scrap and speed production."

Luca asked, "That's a great story. What are some typical questions we should ask the EB?"

QUESTION TO ASK THE ECONOMIC BUYER

1. Where in your priority list does this particular problem rank?
2. What specific business measure does this issue most effect?
3. When would you prefer to solve this issue?
4. Would you be willing to allocate budget? E.g., if we could prove during the Validation Event that we could save your company $*X* for an investment of $*Y*, would you allocate $*Y* budget?
5. Besides yourself, is there anyone else required to approve a purchase of this size?
6. If we are successful in the POV, what would be the remaining steps in your decision process?

WHAT IS THE ECONOMIC BUYER GOING TO ASK ME?

Luca, a manager from Italy, who used to sell frozen foods but was hired because of his brain power and off-the-charts drive, asked, "What will the Economic Buyer ask me?"

"Great question, Luca!" I told them that the general questions Economic Buyers almost always ask fall into four groups:

Much-ness
Soon-ness
Sure-ness
Easy-ness.

"So," I said as I grabbed the dry-erase marker again. "Help me build this out. What questions should fall under each category?"

Much-ness:

- How much does it cost?
- How much does it cost to implement?
- How much will the customer save?

Soon-ness:

- How soon can the solution be implemented?
- How soon before the company sees a return on their investment?"

Sure-ness:

- How sure are you that your product will work in their environment?

- How sure are you of the cost justification?
- Which one of your customers can the customer speak with to be sure?

Easy-ness:

- How easy is it to implement?
- How easy is it for the company's people to learn how to use it?

Most of the time, before the meeting adjourns, an Economic Buyer will ask if you have any final questions for them. For me, there is one final question I like to ask before I leave their office:

Would it be OK to call you under only two conditions?

1. If we find that our final business case is materially different then the preliminary justification after the validation event.
2. If anyone decides to significantly change our agreed validation criteria.

These conditions set the stage to show a final cost justification after any material discoveries during the validation event and, most importantly, to prevent the competition and their Champion from trying to change the criteria in their favor.

I especially like to stress the second condition if the competitions' Champion is attending the Economic Buyer meeting. That agreement between me and the Economic Buyer places a warning to the competition's Champion to not attempt to change the validation criteria.

Andy raised his hand. "I assume the customer-verifiable exit criteria for the Economic Buyer meeting are easy to define. You either had the meeting or didn't."

"That's right, Andy. The verifiable exit criteria for the next few stages are very tangible. The events either occurred or didn't and if they transpired, did you successfully obtain all the required information to proceed to the next step in the process."

39
THE TREE

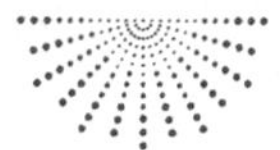

Do you remember me telling you about Carlo, the greatest salesperson I'd ever witnessed? The one who possessed urgent curiosity? I'd like to tell another story about Carlo that emphasizes the importance of always getting high in an account.

Every time I went on sales calls with Carlo, we called on the CEOs of the largest companies in the Emilia Romagna region of Italy, companies like Ferrari, GD, Marchesini, Maserati and Ducati.

Carlo always got to the CEO in all of his accounts. Now, I was curious.

"How do you consistently call so high?" I asked.

"Think of any organization as a tree," he said. "With the roots at the bottom supporting the trunk, the trunk supporting the branches, and the branches supporting the twigs. All the branches have money. Even the twigs, to some degree, have money to spend. But it's only at the very top of the tree where you find the big money. That's where control of the big money lives.

"Most sales reps make sales calls with the intention of making their way toward the top of the tree. They start at the trunk. When someone is willing to speak with them, they walk out on one of the low-level branches. After speaking with multiple people on the branch, and a maybe a few of the twigs, they now want to travel up the tree.

"At this point, most reps get blocked by an enemy or insecure manager, who doesn't want the rep to go over their head. Sometimes they're blocked from going higher by the competitor's Champion, who wants to control the decision criteria and process. Other times, the installed base Champion doesn't want to lose their status and control, so they prevent the rep from calling higher. The bottom branches of the tree are fraught with roadblocks."

The metaphor made perfect sense. Strung out on the lower branches of the tree, the rep feels they have lost control.

They're boxed in.

They see the decision criteria outlined for the competitor's product and the process moving without their input.

It's clear that the competition has a Champion and is controlling the sale. The rep thinks about pulling out of the process, because he knows he's already lost. But the competition's Champion threatens him that if he pulls out, he and his company will never do business with the company ever again.

Eighty percent of the time, the trapped rep capitulates, tries to educate the customer and does a POV dreaming of finding a Champion during the POV in the hope of changing the criteria.

Vain attempt.

Once the rep is told they lost the deal, the rep has an unrealistic expectation that their manager, their CRO, or even their CEO can, late in the process, call into the top branches of the tree and help change the decision.

But the reps are all completely trapped. No way out . . . they just don't realize it.

Because the rep's presentation of the solution to the lower-level managers educated the lower-level managers, those managers can now compare and contrast the differences between the solutions.

Skew the results.

Protecting their personal wins

Then the Economic Buyer tells the sales manager, CEO, or CRO that he'll investigate. He calls his lower-level managers who seem to have done their homework on selecting the best solution. They're well prepared to share their evaluation criteria. The Economic Buyer is impressed with the diligent work of his team and informs the sales manager, CEO, or CRO of their final decision.

The frustrated manager, livid at the news of losing a brand name account, tells the Economic Buyer that it was an unfair process in which the decision criteria were manipulated and controlled. Controlled by the competition and a biased employee, who is the competition's Champion.

At this point, any experienced Economic Buyer asks the manager just one very simple question, "Did your rep agree to participate in the POV, knowing the decision criteria?"

"Yes."

The clever Economic Buyer will respond by saying, "It sounds like you got outsold."

The competitor won.

It's over.

"The key," Carlo said, "is to start higher in the tree."

High in the tree is where the big money lives. High in the tree is where the people who control the money live. High in the tree is where big business problems are discussed. By starting high, you gain a huge advantage over the competition, since most competitors don't climb high in the tree until it's too late.

But Carlo also said, "Be aware: As you climb the tree, you need to understand that there's a different language spoken up there. Speak on their business terms. Take the time to understand their business and the business problem you are solving."

Speaking in business terms meanings hitting topics like increased revenues, decreased costs, improved margins, productivity, limit risks, time to market, and increased market share. If you don't understand their business, you won't solve a big business problem. If don't you speak in their business terms, ***they will relegate you to the lower branches*** **of the tree.**

"I've definitely seen many reps start low in organizations and get boxed in by the competition's champion or an insecure manager when they tried calling higher," Andy said. "That illustrated it perfectly."

From the side, Luca groaned. "It's such a true story! I've participated in POVs where we lost, then asked Raj to call the Economic Buyer late in the process, but it never works because we already did the POV."

"The outcomes could easily go differently if reps find pain *above the noise* and high-level Champions to get them to the EB," said Jim.

"That's right Jim," I said. "It's especially true in any replacement sale. The competition already has a Champion protecting the installed base. The person who originally purchased the competitor's product will typically fight to keep you on the low branches and your product out of the account."

"Why does someone do that?" asked Stevie Mac.

"Because they are invested in their personal status within the account. When they bought the competitors product, they received a win—recognition, control, approval, promotion, etc. —and they will fight to protect the stature they gained."

40
SALES MANAGER ADVICE

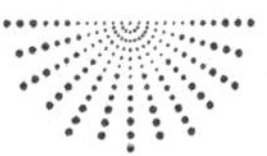

As I gathered my things to leave the conference room, Jim approached me with a warm smile and a handshake. "Hey, John. Can we meet for a drink at the pool cabana outside the casino? I'd like to ask you a few questions about issues I've run into."

"Sure."

We stepped out into a beautiful, sunny seventy-two-degree February day in Las Vegas. (The desert isn't all that bad in the winter.) I sat down and ordered a Harpoon IPA. He ordered one also.

As the waiter walked away, Jim leaned his long arms onto his legs and gave me a somewhat troubled look. "As we've learned new things as a management team," he said, "it's become uncomfortable implementing change on my team. Most of my reps are either slow to change or are resisting change. I've tried coaching, yelling, probing, cajoling, but they aren't changing when they go into accounts. Do you have any advice for me?"

"Jim, right now, it's more comfortable for your reps to not change. If you want to create change you need to '*make it rain.*' Let me tell you a story about that."

GRAY BOY

One beautiful spring night in Boston when the leaves on trees were growing, the smell of budding flowers in the air, and the birds were singing, I planned to go out to dinner and the movies with my wife. After work, I entered the house, greeted my wife and kids, and ran upstairs to take a shower.

After showering and dressing, I returned downstairs.

My wife said, "We're not going to the movies."

Gray Boy, the family cat, was stuck in a tree.

I said, "Well, he'll eventually come down. Have you called the fire department?"

"Of course. They don't get cats out of trees."

"Well, he'll get tired or hungry, and he'll eventually come down. Let's go to the movies."

"Cats don't come down from trees," my wife said.

"That's strange. I don't know of any stories of dead cats falling out of trees, so the cats must eventually find a way to come down."

She stared at me expectantly.

Realizing I was at an impasse with my wife, I sighed and said, "Show me where Gray Boy is."

Gray Boy comfortably sat halfway up the largest oak tree in my yard. It towered over the roof of my house. My house had a walkout from the basement into the backyard and a staircase that led to a porch on the first floor. Thinking that cats hate water, I had the idea that I might be able to force Gray Boy down from the tree by spraying water over his head.

I would create a little pain for Gray Boy.

So, I went down to the backyard, grabbed the water hose, pulled it up the stairs to the porch, and tried to spray into the tree above where Gray Boy sat.

The moment he heard the noise of the water spray, he darted higher into the tree to avoid getting wet.

Okay, I thought. *If he's going higher, I have to go higher.*

I brought my ladder over, climbed onto the roof with the hose, and tried to spray above Gray Boy with the same result. Gray Boy, quick as lightning, climbed to the very top of the tree, where he slowly swayed on the thin branches.

"I give up!" I called to my wife and climbed back down from the roof. When I put the ladder away, Gray Boy still swayed in the tree. I wondered if he would stay in those thin branches if wind swirled up.

"The weather forecast said it's going to be windy and rainy tonight. When Gray Boy is wet and hungry, he'll find his way down."

She reluctantly agreed, and we left for the movie.

We returned home at 10:00 p.m. I grabbed a flashlight and shined it on the oak tree. Gray Boy was still sitting high up in the branches.

My wife's brow furrowed. "He's never going to come down."

"I'm done. I'm going to bed. Don't worry. Gray Boy will be down from the tree in the morning."

When I woke at 6:00 a.m. the next day, it was cloudy and raining, and the temperature had dropped. Gray Boy stood on the back porch with his nose one centimeter from the sliding glass door that led into the warm kitchen, which housed food and water. There he sat wet, cold, tired, hungry, and uncomfortable (his pains). Only the glass door prevented Gray Boy from exiting pain and finding pleasure.

We're all just like Gray Boy.

We all will do almost anything to avoid pain and anything to seek pleasure. When Gray Boy was in the tree, it was more comfortable to continue up the tree than face his fear and risk climbing down. Only when he crossed the tipping point of pain in the pain/pleasure dynamic was he willing to come down from the tree and into more pleasurable circumstances.

In this way, people are no different than Gray Boy.

They gravitate toward pleasure and do anything to avoid pain. As leaders, we need to understand the *pleasure/pain dynamic*. It's our job to create an environment where it's more pleasurable for reps to ask the customers the difficult qualifying questions, explore deeper during Discovery, and examine the details during Scoping. Otherwise, they'll face the pain of the tough account and qualification questions *you* will constantly ask.

"Jim," I said as he mused on the story, "many first-time sales leaders don't want to 'make it rain' by asking their reps basic, difficult questions. They wait until it's too late to ask. Why? Because it's more pleasurable for managers to *not* ask the difficult questions until they don't have the answers for why their forecast is falling apart at the end of the quarter. Then, when the managers cross into the pain of a disintegrating forecast, it becomes more pleasurable to ask the questions.

"If you want to develop your reps, ask the tough questions early in the quarter. If you don't develop them by constantly asking painful deal-qualification and sales-process questions, then your reps will never find it more pleasurable to dig deeper into the sales process and ask customers the more difficult sales-process questions."

When I say, "causing pain," I don't mean yelling or screaming, because that creates an intolerable work environment. What I am referring to is being consistent in training your reps by continually asking them qualification questions when they return from a sales call without you. Over time, they'll understand the pain of continually facing you without the answers to your account questions. They'll find pleasure in developing the courage and skill to ask the customer the questions.

MIRROR OF REALITY

Jim said, "Sometimes people bring me different account issues. I can sense that they may be emotional, they may leave out information, they may stretch the truth, or they may simply bring me bad news. How should I deal with that?"

"You are paid to be the *mirror of reality*. You need to quickly understand the reality of situations by boring to the core of the issue. Don't be afraid to stare the reality of potentially very bad news directly in the eyes."

Only through effective listening skills, zero emotional bias, and great probing questions will you need in order to be able to truly understand what's happening.

The situation is what it is. Don't bias yourself and let other opinions make you believe circumstances are something other than what they are. You're paid to understand the cold, hard truth of the matter. You are paid to be the mirror of reality.

Deal with it.

Deal with it NOW.

DON'T BE IN A HURRY TO MAKE A MISTAKE

Jim said, "Many times, people call me or come into my office informing me of a situation. Usually, there's a long, back-and-forth discussion where they present the details and I ask questions to get additional information. After all my questions, they look at me and ask, 'So, what should we do?' I feel pressured to make a decision as if I'm the answer man,"

"If it's not an urgent matter with high stakes, don't be in a hurry to make a mistake. Few times are you actually required to make an immediate decision. If I don't know the answer, I'll say, 'I don't know. I hear what you're saying, and I understand it, but I can't feel it.'

"That typically gets them to ask, 'What do you mean?' And I can explain how my head understands the situation, but something in my gut tells me to wait to make the decision. If they ask, 'when will you know?' my answer is simply 'I don't know.'

"The answers for difficult questions could come at any time. I could be driving home, on a run, or taking a shower, but I'll know when my head matches my gut. It will come to me, and it's always right. But if I didn't give myself enough time to mull over the question, I could have made a mistake by giving a hasty answer. So, if you don't feel like a decision is the right one, wait.

Sit on it. Take your time. Make the decision when you know it's the right decision."

TWO BUCKETS

Jim moved on and asked, "Many of my reps focus on things outside our control, like product enhancements, the quality of leads from Marketing or other company issues. I wind up getting defocused from the most important issues."

"For sales leaders, there are two big buckets in any company," I said. "There's the 'control' bucket and the 'no control' bucket. One bucket is for the things you can control, and the other bucket is for the things you can't control.

"Stop worrying about things that aren't in your control. The things you and your team can't change. Your focus should be on the things you can control, like recruiting the best people, onboarding new recruits, finding ways to increase training for your reps, developing your people's skills, and leading your team. Focus on working diligently to make all the things under your control world class."

I continued, "There is nothing worse than leaders that make excuses for their team's performance based on the things they can't control. Trying to point the finger at something or someone else. It's a poor excuse for non-performance."

"So, what you're really telling me is that I need to change," said Jim.

"Exactly. It all starts with you, the leader. You need to get comfortable doing things you've never done before. Get comfortable being uncomfortable."

COMFORTABLE BEING UNCOMFORTABLE

There are moments in life when someone says a phrase that narrows into something we may have felt or experienced many times but couldn't put into words.

I sat a board meeting at a startup company located in San Francisco's financial district, just a few blocks off Market Street. At the head of the table sat Sam Vigor, managing partner at Tree Top Capital.

I sat to Sam's right, and he asked question after question about the startup business presented by the CRO and the CEO.

At one point, the CEO described a situation in which he was completely uncomfortable. He'd never been in a startup. He had never before experienced anything like his current scenario.

After listening intently, Sam responded by telling the team that, "If you're going to be in a startup, you need to get comfortable being uncomfortable."

When I heard Sam say the words *comfortable being uncomfortable*, it resonated right through my bones, my heart, and into my soul. I could feel those words coursing through my veins.

I thought back to the many startups I had been in and how many times I had been completely uncomfortable. I'd been in situations that I had never before experienced. Situations in which I needed to search for the best solution (or what seemed like the best solution), to my predicament. Situations in which I'd needed the courage to take decisive action immediately.

Those situations forced me to get out of my comfort zone, because I couldn't rely on experience to tell me what to do. I couldn't rely on anyone else to help me. I could only rely on my instincts and the little data I had.

Sam's comments took me back to my first startup, when faced with an issue I had never seen before. I went to see my CEO, Dick, to ask for advice. After I laid out the situation, I asked Dick, "What do you think we should do?"

Dick immediately answered, "How the f*ck should I know? You and I have never done this before."

At first, I stared at him, startled into silence.

But then I thought about the genuineness of his answer in admitting that he didn't know.

"Figure it out," he said. "Make the best decision you can with the information you have. And use your gut. Your best instincts. If it turns out you made the wrong decision, change it quickly. Don't get married to your decisions. Don't tie your ego to your decisions."

In other words, I needed to step up.

Get comfortable making uncomfortable decisions.

Powerful advice that guided me for many years, and something that Jim needed now. I could see the hesitancy and uncertainty in his eyes. He thought he needed his team to approve of these changes to the sales process, but he didn't.

He needed to take control. To let go of whatever he held onto that kept him from truly leading his team. He needed to get comfortable as the leader. It was time to step up.

NOT A POPULARITY CONTEST

"So, you're saying it's good to be uncomfortable?" Jim asked.

"No, I'm saying you need to get comfortable being a leader. Comfortable doing things you haven't done before. I think you're trying to stay in your comfort zone," I countered. "Seems to me you want everything needed to help your team do better, *and* you want to stay comfortable. You want to make sure you're winning a popularity contest. Jim, this is not a popularity contest."

Based on the way he fidgeted, I could tell I'd hit a nerve.

"Not everyone will like you, and that's OK," I continued. "You're not going to get an award for being popular. The job of the sales leader is about maximizing bookings by recruiting the best people, training and developing people, holding them accountable to standards of performance, getting individuals to perform as a cohesive team, and creating a culture of competence to help people win. By implementing these changes we've discussed, that's exactly what you would be doing."

Jim nodded slowly.

"I'm sure you discovered some of these things as captain of your hockey team at Wisconsin," I pointed out as I leaned back in my chair. "To make changes and implement a new sales process, you can't make decisions on whether or not you'll be liked. You'll need to make some unpopular decisions, which means you may not be the most popular person with all your team members. That's OK, because if people believe *you have their best interests at heart*, if they are becoming more competent because of your coaching and vested interest in them, they're not going to leave you."

"I get what you're saying," he said with a sigh. "I can't worry about being popular, but I want my team to know that I care for them."

"That's perfectly fine. Your people should know that you care," I said, "but how do you show people you care?"

"I'm not exactly sure."

41
CARING THROUGH COMPETENCE

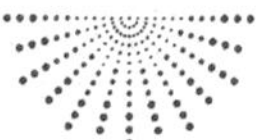

In one company I advised, the CEO and COO started every meeting with a hug for everyone. They believed that if they hugged people, it made people feel good and sent an unspoken message that they cared about their employees.

But the attrition rate at the company was the highest I'd ever seen at any startup company.

Why?

Because the huggers never trained and developed their people. Because caring is deeper than hugging. A hug is temporary.

Caring is about competence.

Competence is forever.

You show you care when you take the time to become intimate with your people, understand their strengths and weaknesses and dedicate your efforts to training people and developing their knowledge and skills, so they can succeed in their jobs and their careers. Making your people competent is truly caring for your people.

I'm sure you've heard the saying, "People don't leave companies, they leave managers."

Throughout the ups and downs of a company, people won't leave if they believe their manager cares. They know their manager cares because their manager dedicates time and effort to help make their employees competent.

COMPETENCE DRIVES WINNING

Many company leaders believe that by providing things like ping pong tables, bean bag chairs, beer taps, and foosball tables in their facilities, they have created a good workplace culture.

Don't get me wrong: games and socializing definitely add to an endurable work environment. Those things allow everyone to break up the monoDan of the daily grind, but they certainly don't make a *culture*.

The roots of a truly positive workplace culture lie in helping people win and achieve their personal goals.

Reps want to be trained and developed. They want to grow. They want to be in a stimulating environment where everyone is winning, growing, and developing.

When people win, they learn, develop, grow, make money and get promoted. That's an engaging workplace culture. THAT is a culture that no one wants to leave. And that's a culture people want to join.

On the flip side, if people aren't winning, learning, earning and growing, they're not going to stick around a workplace culture, for hugs and the ping pong table.

PRIDE IS WHAT PEOPLE WANT

Pride is what people really want.

They want to be proud of the job they do. Proud of their increasing competence. Proud of the people they work with. Proud of the product they sell and proud of their company.

The only way to achieve an environment of pride starts with the leader doing whatever possible to help people win.

Pride is what people want.

Winning is the precursor to pride.

Competence is the precursor to winning.

Caring means making people competent.

YOU OWN IT. TAKE RESPONSIBILITY

One issue that I see as reps' transition to sales manager is their hesitancy to take ownership of their new role. If they show hesitation here, their team will sense it. Issues will follow, which is exactly what Jim started to experience.

"The sales manager is the leader," I said to Jim. "Own that title. You are responsible for everything that happens with your people, your accounts, your forecast, and your bookings. The performance of your team is a direct reflection on your leadership. Take ownership. If *you* don't own it, *who* does?"

"I understand everything you have said. It all makes sense. But how should I analyze performance issues as we make these changes?" Jim asked.

"As you approach any individual on a performance issue, first, ask yourself if this is a time for you to manage or to lead?" "Second, ask yourself, *are my people competent and committed*?"

"What's the difference?"

"*Competence* speaks to the knowledge and skills for success in the job. The WHAT they need to know and the HOW they need to do things.

"*Commitment* addresses the individual will, motivation, and drive to consistently perform at their highest level. The WHY they need to do things."

Jim nodded slowly. "OK, that's interesting way to look at it. Most of the time I just think they're not trying hard enough or don't have enough grit, but I haven't approached performance issues from both an ability and dedication standpoint."

When addressing a performance issue, leave your emotions at home. Don't be biased. Drive down a line of questioning to determine whether this a competence issue or a commitment issue.

Competence issue = Speak to their head. This will be more of a ***fact-finding*** discussion. It will lead to and understanding of **WHAT** they should know and **HOW** they should do things.

Here are some questions to get it going:

- At what specific step and stage of the sales process are they failing and why?
- What knowledge are they lacking?
- If it is knowledge, is there a training class that can improve their knowledge?
- Do they have the intelligence to comprehend the material?

- Are they failing because of a skill issue?
- If it is a skillset, can you, another manager, or another rep work with them to develop the skill?
- Are you competent in the area they are failing so you can help them?

Commitment issue = Speak to their heart. This is more of a ***feeling-finding*** discussion. It will lead to you generating an understanding of **WHY** they should do things.

Here are a few questions to get you started:

- Why do they feel their performance is low?
- If they always have been committed, what has changed?
- Has something changed in their personal life?
- Are you motivating them?
- Are they bored and need a new challenge?
- Are they adapting to the changing sales environment?"
- Is someone or something demotivating them?
- Do they have the desire to learn new material?
- Are they coachable?

Think about it like this:

Managers tell me to do things by speaking to my head.

Leaders motivate me to do things by speaking to my heart.

After I laid out a path, confidence returned to Jim's expression. He nodded more firmly this time.

"You're right," he said. "I'm the leader. I have some members of my team who have issues, but I have one rep with a competency issue. When and how do you determine that someone won't make it and should be asked to leave?"

"It's always a difficult choice and many times you'll struggle with the decision. You were the one who hired this person, right?"

"Yes."

"Then, you thought they met your *position description* at the time of hiring, correct?"

"Yes."

"If that's the case, then you were responsible for their development."

"Yes, that's true."

"That means that *anytime you have to terminate a rep, it's a reflection on you. You either hired the wrong rep or you hired the right rep and couldn't develop them.* In either case, it's important for you to analyze what you did wrong and make adjustments, so you don't repeat the mistake." It was time to get him to reflect. "In this particular case, what do you think you missed?"

"The rep has been here for one year and hasn't ever made quota, his pipeline is always weak, he doesn't completely understand our product or differentiators, and he's never fully prepared for a meeting."

"What do you think the real issue is?", I questioned.

"I can't put my finger on it, but I'll utilize the competence-commitment questioning to get to the issue."

"I don't want to bias you, but it sounds like you may have a both commitment and competence issues", I said.

"That's what my instinct told me but why do you say that?"

"The rep has been here a year, if they were intelligent, they'd fully comprehend your product but not showing up prepared for meetings is a commitment issue. It's lack of drive, lack of motivation. It comes down to character traits.", I said.

I continued, "It always does. If they don't have the intelligence, they won't learn your product. If they don't have the drive, they won't develop the job skills, which, in this case, may be affecting pipeline development and meeting preparation."

"You'll need to decide if you made a hiring mistake or there is something standing in the way of this rep getting on track."

"OK, I feel ready to address performance issues." said Jim, sounding relieved.

I clapped him on the shoulder. "You're doing a great job, Jim."

42
VALIDATION EVENT

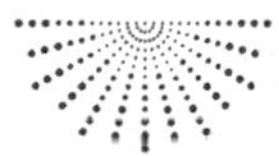

The next morning, I opened the discussion on validation events with a question.

"Let's pretend I'm asking all of you to compete in a sporting event on Saturday afternoon at the local high school. Each of you needs to compete, and each competitor must wager $1,000. Winner takes all. Any questions?"

A flurry of questions came at me.

"What are the competitive events?"

"Should I bring my track shoes, football shoes, hockey skates, basketball shoes, or baseball shoes?" Jim asked.

"What equipment should I bring?"

"How are the competitions scored?" Luca asked, following up with the predictable, "I want to understand how to win."

"How many competitions are there?"

I laughed. "Good job. You're asking all the right questions. You wouldn't show up and give away $1,000 if you believed the criteria for winning didn't align to your personal athletic strengths, would you?"

"No."

"It's no different in selling. You have to define the POV criteria to ensure alignment with your product strengths. If the criteria are not aligned to your strengths, you won't win the POV. You'll waste your time. You'll lose."

It's critical to define the criteria for the Validation Event so that your differentiators are included. Then, ensure that the scoring for each product capability is weighted in favor of your solution.

When it comes to the validation event, agreeing with the customer on the criteria, the weighting of every element of the criteria, and the scoring of each in writing prior to the event is critical.

WHAT IS A POV (VALIDATION EVENT)?

The Validation Event brings the sales process to a natural conclusion. You either win it (and get the sale) or you lose it (and don't get the sale).

The customer uses the Validation Event to ensure that your product solves their problem.

Hannlin spoke up. "The proof of value validates your solution capabilities to solve their pain and substantiates the metrics in your cost justification."

"Exactly," I said. "The POV substantiates value for the customer, but, as a sales rep, what is the Validation Event for you?"

"It should be a *prelude to an order*," Luca said. "Prior to the Validation Event, you have *confirmed with the EB* that the customer is committed to buy if the test is successful."

"Correct Luca. It's quid pro quo. You agreed with the Economic Buyer, prior to the validation event, that the winner will receive a purchase order subject only to legal review and pricing negotiation."

What a Validation Event Is NOT

The Validation Event is NOT:

- An event which occurs *early* in the sales process
- A time to educate the customer on your product
- An opportunity to start discovering pain
- A chance to find a Champions
- A time to make friends

Only Perform a Validation Event After:

- You have a confirmed Champion.
- Your Champion has helped you frame the validation criteria and scoring rules for the POV.
- From your Discovery and Scoping findings, you and your Champion have built a cost justification where the gain far exceeds the pain.
- You verified the priority, budget, authority, timing, and remaining process steps with the Economic Buyer.

"What were you doing wrong on your past validation events (POVs)?" I asked.

Jim said, "Never understanding that the rep who controls the test criteria wins."

Andy followed shortly after, "Without proper Discovery and Scoping, we couldn't find and build a Champion and we never could align our product to POV criteria."

"Plus," Jim added, "we didn't meet with the EB prior to the POV to finalize the criteria and understand if the pain we discovered was a priority for the company to solve."

"Or gained agreement from the EB that they would allocate budget and buy after a successful POV. We were just blindly pushing for a POC." Luca added

WHAT SHOULD REPS DO DURING VALIDATION EVENTS?

Reps should be ready during Validation Events to do the following:

- Reconfirm the *as-is* and *to-be* process metrics from the cost justification.
- Adjust the *as-is* and *to-be* processes based on new information.
- Capture material evidence of the solution solving the customer's pain.
- Continue to align to the Champions' personal win

WHAT TO DO AFTER THE VALIDATION EVENT

"What should you do *after* the Validation Event happens?" I asked.

Stevie Mac quickly said, "We need to build a summary report of findings and share it, face-to-face, with our Champion. Obtaining buy-in from our Champion is critical to building their confidence to move toward a purchase. We need to ensure the Champion understands and agrees with all elements of the business case. There shouldn't be any doubt."

"And if our results materially change our original cost justification, incorporate those results into a new justification to share with the EB to further justify our price and drive urgency," Luca said.

They were really starting to get it now.

43

BUSINESS CASE

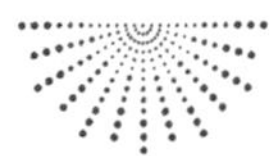

"Let's keep going and discuss the Business Case," I said to the group. "It's the fifth step and flows right after the Validation Event. Someone tell me what it is?"

Luca raised his hand. "A Business Case is the formal, face-to-face presentation of the final results to the Economic Buyer."

"It's their *value realization document*," Andy said. "It provides the potential gain over pain details, which are consistent with your findings throughout Discovery, Scoping, Economic Buyer meetings, and the Validation Event."

The Business Case should be thought of as the customer's internal document rather than the vendor's document. Write the business case from their perspective—as if they wrote it.

It should include everything you need for the meeting:

- Their *corporate objectives*
- Their *strategic initiatives*
- The *business problem or opportunity*

- How their problem or opportunity fits into meeting their strategic initiatives
- Descriptions of the *before and after* use-case scenarios with an explanation of how your solution uniquely solves the business problem
- An explanation on how your solution delivers the business outcome with the people, processes, and timeframes to solve the problem/achieve the goals
- A *final cost justification* that translates the quantifiable benefits of your solution into business value in the Economic Buyer's terms. (i.e., revenue, margin, risks, time to market, market share, production costs, etc.)

Take note: you can't express the value only in general terms, like increased productivity, reduced headcount, quicker time to market, etc. without adding a material measure or a quantified value.

Express the Business Case in the particular way your customer expresses business value. The results have to be *translated into their business terms*. For instance, increase annual revenue by twenty million dollars, eliminate fifty million dollars in production scrap, decrease XYZ product time to market by ten percent, resulting in fifteen million dollars of cost savings, etc.

Your Business Case becomes the post-implementation baseline for measuring the success of your solution. *It should establish a baseline for comparison to actual post-implementation results.*

Measuring positive results after the implementation will allow you to justify additional purchases and establish credibility to potentially cross-sell new products.

BUYER RISK

The buyer's risk reaches its highest-level right after the Validation Event, when the buyer is faced with the reality of making a final buying decision. Their fear of making the wrong decision climbs. They worry about their standing in the organization and a loss of power from Championing a product that may not work.

A good business case will help them through their fear to take a leap of faith.

"What do our reps have to do to overcome that risk?" Jim asked. "How can we help them be successful at this most critical stage?"

A number of things can help:

- Remind them of the results from the Validation Event, which proved that the product works to solve pains in their use case.
- Mention the negative consequences of not solving their pains.
- Share common results from other customers who have had the same pains.
- Have them speak to a Champion at another company who had positive results.
- Remind them of their personal win and how this purchase will allow them to achieve an overall win.

"You also need to present an Implementation Plan," I said. "A well-thought-out Implementation Plan decreases risk and increases the odds of achieving the success outlined in the Business Case. You're highlighting the resources available to support the customer in the vein of ensuring their success."

"It can also create urgency for the purchase," Luca said.

I grabbed my dry-erase marker and tossed it to Stevie Mac. "Write down a typical scenario to drive prioritization for the buy."

He wrote out a typical template to use in order to create urgency:

1. *Start a project on (A DATE)*
2. *Train (STAKEHOLDERS) by (B DATE)*
3. *Reserve any internal resources for required services for (C DATE)*
4. *Arrange all of this within the (TIMEFRAME) the Economic Buyer established in order to achieve the results by (D DATE)*
5. *Finalize contract by (Z DATE) so required resources can be reserved and deadline can be met.*

44
NEGOTIATE AND CLOSE

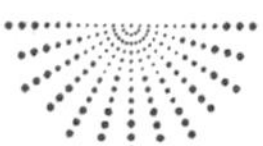

"Let's say you get a deal past the Validation Event, and you're excited," I said as Stevie Mac took his seat again. "That ushers you into the sixth and final step of the B2B sales process: Negotiate and Close."

I heard a couple of low-level cheers.

"Don't get excited yet. You still have some hurdles ahead," I told the group.

PROCUREMENT

In most organizations, for deals over a certain dollar size, the Procurement Department gets involved to negotiate better pricing and payment terms. In many organizations, Procurement is measured and obtains a bonus on their ability to discount the pricing proposal you as the sales rep gave to the business.

To gain pricing leverage, Procurement will essentially perform a *virtual separation of the business side of the company from the procurement side*. This separation is used in an effort to *isolate the price of your product from any measurable business value* you created in an effort to commoditize your product.

They may also put a "gag order" on business communications with you. That prevents your Champion and the Economic Buyer from giving you any further information until Procurement is done negotiating price. Even if Procurement speaks to your Champion or the Economic Buyer, and they both express their interest in only having your solution, Procurement still has a job to perform, *decrease your price.*

Meanwhile, Procurement will try to gain pricing leverage by creating a bidding war. They will invite price quotations from your closest competitors. In most large organizations, Procurement is required to obtain price quotations from two to three different competitors for any major purchase. When Procurement requests a proposal from one of your competitors in an effort to decrease your price, it's an alarm to a smart competitor. When an intelligent competitor, not actively engaged with an account, receives an incoming call from the account Procurement Department, they instantly recognize they are late in the sales process and need to act quickly to have any chance of winning.

Your competitor's goal will be to delay the deal and buy time to perform a shortened sales process of their own. With Procurement's approval, the competitor will identify and call the Economic Buyer to delay the sale. Your competitor will plant fear, uncertainty, and doubt regarding your product offering. They'll try to create distrust in your company, hoping the Economic Buyer will take time to consider an alternative solution. At a minimum, they will heavily discount their price in an effort to "steal the deal".

That is why you don't skip steps.

This is where salespeople who didn't perform the sales process correctly are most at risk. It's the critical reason you needed to quantify pain and associated-business benefits early in the process, linking them to your unique differentiation in a cost justification.

If you don't have a Champion or haven't agreed on a cost justification with the Economic Buyer, you're in jeopardy of completely losing the deal or, at a minimum, taking a significant cut to your pricing proposal, because the customer will justify price based on either *their perceived value* of your solution or the *lowball offer from your competitor.*

STRENGTH DURING NEGOTIATION

"In all this hair-raising process, what do you have as an asset to close your sale?" I asked.

Several hands shot into the air.

"Your strength comes from the decision criteria you created which any new competitor will be judged by," Andy said.

"Proof of your unique differentiation solving their pains in the validation event," Jim said.

Stevie Mac piped up, "You justified your price and *set a price anchor* based on your cost justification after an acknowledgement from the EB."

Luca leaned back in his chair. "All of those items are certainly necessary but the main reason you have strength is because *you've established trust and maintained a positive business relationship with the Champion and Economic Buyer*, making it difficult for any competitor to establish the same level of trust in a short timeframe. Without the relationship with the EB and Champion, you have no power."

In other words, you have a seat at the table. The competitor does not. They're late to the process. You're in control. The only way for them to get Procurement's attention is to throw out a lowball-price offer. If you haven't skipped steps, the customer will understand why they need to buy from you at your justified price point.

PROCUREMENTS' TECHNIQUES

There are many different plans of attack that Procurement Departments have utilized. Here are just a few, of the many techniques I've experienced and you certainly will:

1. **The "pissed off for no apparent reason" approach:** Even if I've just introduced myself for the first time and they don't even know me, they act pissed off, because I did a good job selling to their organization. As if they want to say, "I'm pissed off that you've been talking to the business and gave us a small discount. Aren't you embarrassed?"
2. **The "take it or leave it" offer:** Procurement may try to say something like this, "We never pay this much money for software. We did an enterprise license deal with Microsoft for a fifty percent discount. Your company is not Microsoft. We demand a seventy-percent discount. Take it or leave it."
3. **The "you need us more than we need you" brush off:** "Every sales rep wants use our logo and say they have our company as a customer. In return for using our name and logo, we'll need a fifty-percent discount."
4. **The "we love you" charade:** "Our team has really loved working with you. I've been told that you've been a tremendous asset during this process. However, I'm sure, as much as they love you, this deal won't go

through at this price point. You'll need to do much better on price."

5. **The "no budget" bust:** "I don't know why the Economic Buyer told you he could pay $500,000, because he only has $150,000 in his budget. I checked with my boss, and no one can change that."
6. **The "good guy/bad guy" setup:** "I won't consider taking a high price quote like this into the VP Procurement's office. You'll have to sharpen your pencil before I'm going to get embarrassed by my boss with your offer."
7. **The "disappearing friend" act:** This person gives you their mobile number; asks about your family and shares information about theirs; talk sports, competition, and other topics; becomes your friend. Then they string you out until the last hours of the quarter, never responsive to your calls and emails.
8. **The "shame" game:** "All software vendors do is sell the same software product to multiple companies. You're printing money, and you should be ashamed that you're charging us an exorbitant price."
9. **The "one more thing" strategy:** Just when you thought you were done negotiating through all their tricks, there's always one more thing. "I can get this through in the next twenty minutes *if* you'll just throw in training."
10. **The "have a heart" scheme:** "You know the depressed economy has caused everyone in our company difficulty, right? Have a heart and give us the price we need."
11. **The "it's over" gambit:** "This deal is over. I just sent you an email with the price point we can afford. The email has our purchase order attached. All you need to do is agree to terms and conditions with our Legal Department."

REMAIN CALM

First, when these things happen, remain calm.

If you've performed the sales process correctly, you are a respected partner of the Champion and Economic Buyer, and Procurement knows it. In fact, Procurement typically won't like that you've developed strong price justification leverage over the business.

Remember, that urgency is your friend.

There is urgency for the customer to buy now. Urgency was formulated in Scoping through the implication of pain. You created additional urgency to implement the solution within a specific timeframe during your meeting with the Economic Buyer, and timeframes in your Implementation Plan.

Every day that passes, the customer faces the negative consequences of not remedying their pain, because you have uncovered the *why do I have to buy now.*

"We also anchored our price to the cost justification," Jim said. "The Champion verified the numbers, and the Economic Buyer confirmed approval to move forward based on our justification. There is verified strength in our pricing."

"Exactly," I said. "The customer's value realization is in your Business Case. Stay grounded in the tangible business value of your solution. It's highly unlikely that any competitor will understand their business and create as powerful a Champion and Business Case in a short period of time."

When confronted on price, be patient. You have time. You never have to make an immediate decision on price. You can always "think about it" or "consult with your manager."

You have time.

Their business *doesn't* have time. They have a prioritized need to solve the negative consequences now.

Time has become their enemy.

Time is now your friend.

45
ROLE MODELS

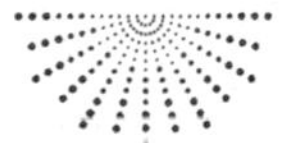

After everyone left the room, Andy and Jim lingered behind.

"Will you join me for a beer?" Andy asked, and looked at Jim as well. "I wanted to get some advice from both of you. We could head over to the Venetian Hotel and maybe talk about. . . Well, I . . . I think I could use some advice on being a role model."

He swallowed hard, and I could tell it took a lot out of him to ask for advice.

"Sure thing," I said.

"I'm interested in helping," Jim said.

Andy nodded in relief while I grabbed my bag. Andy said, "Let's all walk over together."

While we crossed Las Vegas Boulevard, Andy stuffed his hands into his pockets and said, "Through all of this, I've realized that I need to be a better role model for my team. I thought I'd ask about how to do that. I'm not used to really leading. I hate to admit that I'm like a one-trick pony. I'd normally just tell people what to do and get angry if it didn't work out."

"From what I can tell so far," Jim said, "I think the key to our teams' successes is based on our ability to adapt to the new way of selling. I mean, if you and I can't adapt, how can we expect our people to adapt? If you and I aren't the role models for our teams', who will be?"

We crossed into the Venetian and grabbed a table at Majordomo. Andy hadn't said much, but I let Jim speak up. I was curious to see what he'd say, and if it would open up a better relationship between them.

"When I was a captain at Wisconsin," Jim continued, "I eventually learned that every member of the team had a completely different personality. None of them were like me. Each of them needed to be treated differently. They each had different fears, insecurities, motivations, and desires. Only when I got to know them as individuals was I able to inspire them. I also had to help them understand the need to work together as a team for bigger goals."

"How'd you do it?" I asked, anticipating the question in Andy's gaze.

"Group integrity," Jim replied immediately. "On a team, there's nothing more paramount. Your obligation as a leader is to the team and each individual on the team. In turn, each individual's obligation is to the other team members. The leader needs to minimize differences on the team and enforce the motto: *one for all and all for one*. You'll need to do whatever possible to ensure that everyone understands the importance and priority of the team."

"Without it," I said. "You can *lose* your team."

"I've seen that happen," Jim said. "And it can happen *fast.*"

SHOWING UP UNPREPARED

One day, Jim was asked by one of Forego's managers for his feedback on a situation involving a new rep. Apparently, the manager had told all the sales reps to come to the next team meeting prepared to discuss one account plan in detail with the entire team. The new rep showed up late to the meeting and had no prepared account plan.

"What did you do when the new rep showed up without the plan?" Jim asked.

The manager said, "I didn't do anything, but I think he feels bad about it."

In utter disbelief Jim said, "You think he feels bad? Since the account plan meeting, have you ever discussed the situation with the new rep?"

"No."

Jim's story flabbergasted even me, so I took it a step further. "Imagine if you were a hockey coach and a new player on the team showed up late to practice without a stick and helmet," I said, "don't you think the other players would wonder why the new teammate was late? Imagine all of the players' disbelief as the new player skates onto the ice without his helmet and stick."

"The teammates would be upset," Andy said.

"Exactly. If the coach never holds anyone accountable to basic standards, never disciplines the new player, the other players will contemplate whether or not this is the right coach for their team. They would certainly question whether or not the new player was someone special. If this is a team, why would any one individual deserve special treatment?"

"So that leader lost the integrity of the team," Andy said. "And, if the leader isn't acting on behalf of the greater good of the team, that leader will only have a set of individuals who will never attain the greatness of a cohesive team."

"Exactly."

Andy let out a long breath. "You're right. I need to set a few standards of performance for my team and establish minimum operating standards."

"More importantly, you'll need to hold the player accountable, or you'll lose the high performing members of your team."

NON-NEGOTIABLES

"Yes." Jim nodded. "I call my minimum operating standards the "non-negotiables". Here's an analogy, my kids understand, without me having to constantly remind them, that they have to make their beds, brush their teeth, go to school, do their homework, go to bed before a certain hour, etc. Similarly, I've told my team that we can't operate as a team if everyone doesn't adhere to a minimum set of operating standards. We've agreed on a long list."

Jim shared just a few examples of the items on that list:

1. Show up to meetings on time.
2. Always be prepared.
3. Show respect to other team members.
4. Consistently give 100 percent effort.
5. Forecast updates to CRM system every Friday by 5:00 p.m.

6. Obtain required knowledge to understand and articulate needed variables such as
7. The top competitive solution differentiators
8. The competitors' top differentiators
9. The buyers' top pain points and business issues
10. Three customer success stories with dollar metrics
11. Top three customer value drivers for our solution
12. Be able to skillfully present product knowledge such as:
13. The corporate overview
14. Thirty-second elevator pitch
15. A flawless whiteboard pitch
16. Answers to the top-ten most common objections
17. A list of the top-ten Discovery questions
18. A list of the top-ten Scoping questions

"That's really smart, since you can't have a team progress if everyone isn't operating on the same basic principles," Andy said. He nodded a few times as he stared at the wall.

"Andy, Jim is right," I said. "Remember Sly, the smartass fox, and Billy Basics, the hedgehog? You want to simplify your team's focus on the basics. If they can master the basics, you'll need to trust that most everything else will be fine. I would also recommend that you set a few standards of performance but give careful thought to the standards you set."

"Why?"

"Because for any performance standard, you'll need to define clear lines of demarcation for three levels:

Exceptional performance
Acceptable performance
Unacceptable performance

Your entire team will expect to be rewarded for consistent over-achievement, and the performers will expect you to hold the non-performers accountable.

Many leaders set standards of performance but never hold anyone accountable for unacceptable performance. They're quick to celebrate wins for exceptional performance, but they never hold a consistent non-performer on a team accountable.

Their inaction as a leader creates a culture where non-performers know there is no penalty for mediocrity, and the A-list players are disgusted by their leader's inaction to hold people accountable.

Every day that goes by in which the leader doesn't hold the non-performers accountable, the leader, in essence, is penalizing the performers. The top performers want an equitable leader to recognize non-performance as much as performance. When there's no accountability, the top performers question why they should continue to overachieve.

Holding a rep accountable for non-performance can be as simple as taking some territory or accounts away.

That sends a clear message to everyone on the team that you will be rewarded for overachievement and held accountable when you do not perform. This consistent leadership action of reward and accountability will drive a meritocracy within the group and result in team performance increasing over time.

FOCUSING ON NON-PERFORMERS

"I know that some of my non-performers aren't going to make it, but I find myself spending too much of my time trying to help them succeed. Should I continue to spend most of my time with them?" Andy asked.

"It depends on a few factors," I said. And then I told a story of something that had recently happened to me.

I had just finished a four-hour session with executives at a startup company that was doubling bookings every year. I was standing, waiting for the elevator to take me to the lobby, when one of the first-line managers approached me and asked if she could get some advice. I said of course, and we went back inside, found a conference room, and sat down. She asked if I could keep the discussion confidential and told me about her predicament.

She had six sales reps working for her, all of whom had been with the company over seven quarters. She told me that even though she spent the majority of her time trying to train the under performers, they never seemed to respond to her coaching and training, always repeating the same mistakes.

She showed me her team members' numbers:

Six team members

Four who consistently make or beat their $300K quarterly number, $1.2M annually

Two who consistently under perform at $150K per quarter, $600K annually

We dove into the details of the two non-performers. Their knowledge, skills, experience, and characteristics. I asked her to compare and contrast the non-performers to the performers. She told me that the main difference was that the performers were smart, driven, coachable, and adaptable.

Whereas, the non-performers were also smart, but weren't as driven, appeared coachable, because they always seemed open to her advice. But they never adapted.

They never learned new skills. Never changed their ways. They always fell into the same traps. Time traps, objection-handling traps, competitive traps, pipeline-generation traps.

I asked her how much time she spent coaching the performers versus the non-performers. She told me that eighty percent of her time was spent with the non-performers. The remaining time she spent with the performers was mainly to gather information from them on accounts and forecasts, but she didn't offer them much help in coaching or developing.

So, I asked her, "What would happen if you flipped your time and spent eighty percent with the performers? If you could increase the numbers for the performers by twenty percent, that would mean an additional $60K per rep or $240K additional per quarter for the team. But if somehow, someway you could magically increase the performance of the non-performers by twenty percent, that would only equate to $30K per rep or $60K additional per quarter for the team."

She looked at me like I'd just lifted a boulder off her shoulders. She had total relief in her eyes, and I could tell she knew what her next few moves with her team would be.

"That's really helpful, because I have two non-performers on my team that have been with the company for two years, and I think I made two hiring mistakes," Andy said.

I jumped in. "I appreciate that you want to act quickly Andy but remember that if we have to terminate someone, we first need to ask if we hired the wrong person or as leaders, we failed to develop our people."

"I completely understand." Andy answered.

I asked Jim if I could speak to Andy privately. Jim excused himself and said he'd meet us later for dinner. I told Andy there was one more item I wanted to discuss.

EMOTIONAL PROPRIOCEPTION

"Andy, I'd like to give you some individual advice. If you want to go to the next level in any company, you need to become more aware of the effect you have on others, especially your sales team. I call this emotional proprioception. Are you familiar with the term that many runners use called proprioception?"

"No."

"When a runner runs through the woods, their feet hit rocks, roots, mud, gravel and sand. Over time, through an internal feedback system, an experienced runner learns the affect that their foot pressure has on the different types of terrain. Their feedback system constantly trains their mind, which controls and sensitizes their feet, on how much pressure they can apply to the terrain changes and maintain their speed. Too much pressure and they get stuck in the mud, too little pressure and they slip on the rock gravel."

"John, I get it, but why are you telling me about running?"

"Because like a runner that uses proprioception to gain feedback on the affect that they have on things around them, I want you to start developing your emotional proprioception feedback system. I'd like to see you become intensely aware of the effect your words and actions have on those around you, especially the people that work for you."

Andy responded, "Ahhhhh, OK. That makes a lot of sense. I've never had anyone share that type of feedback with me, so thanks. I'm going to be more cognizant of my interactions."

PART IV
ANALYZING DEAL PROGRESSION

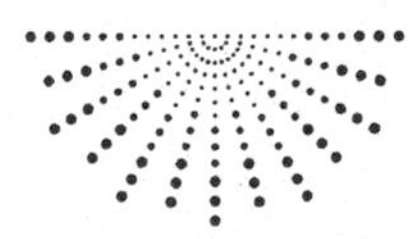

46
ANALYZING SALES EFFECTIVENESS

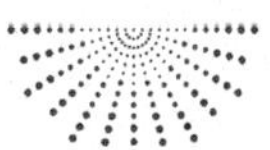

The next morning, the group looked ready to go. Given the many nightly distractions one could find in a city like Las Vegas, I was impressed. Maybe they'd gone to bed early, maybe it was the coffee, maybe it was the oxygen casinos are famous for pumping into the hotel, or maybe it was the ice-cold air conditioning in the room.

Either way, this team was wide awake and wanted to learn.

Even Andy seemed more intent than usual. Computer ready for notes. Talking more easily to his reps. Laughing at a joke.

And Jim seemed to carry his confidence more in his shoulders now.

At this meeting, I needed to move the group from sales process to a qualification methodology. It would allow them to analyze account selling scenarios and understand specifically where they were in the sales process.

In other words, this should drastically change their conversation during the forecasting session at their next QBR.

AN EFFECTIVE ANALYSIS TOOL

"Now, I think you understand a little bit more about why your team needs a sales process," I said, and grinned at a few chuckles. "Not having a sales process is similar to a football coach not having a playbook. Team members are running all over the field without order, without a plan for each player to execute during each and every play of the game. If there's no playbook, winning becomes luck. A non-repeatable event. An art without any proven science."

To determine the effectiveness of each play in the playbook, the coach watches each play during the game and views video replays after the game.

If the coach is intimate with the players' strengths and weaknesses, the coach can accurately assess plays:

The success of each play
What went right and why
What went wrong and where the play went awry
What knowledge or which skill each player may lack to complete a flawless play
The effectiveness of the competition

"Just like a coach, every sales manager needs a sales process (or playbook) that is tightly coupled with a qualification method (analysis capability)," I said. "It helps you analyze the exact status of a deal, what is going right, what is going wrong, and what is the logical next step."

A powerful qualification methodology needs to seamlessly link with your sales process.

Think of a sales process as a Google map.

Imagine you're using Google Maps to drive from Boylston Street on the Boston Common to 59th Street at Central Park South in New York City.

The map would give you turn-by-turn directions that, if followed, would get you from Boston to NYC in the shortest period of time. Similarly, a sales process gives sales reps step-by-step directions that, if followed, will allow someone to obtain an order in the shortest period of time.

But a GPS system works hand-in-hand with Google Maps.

The GPS system gives you the exact status of your location during your drive from Boston to NYC. It gives information on the next turn, distance to your destination, and the time left. If you make a wrong turn, it informs you how to return to the ideal route to NYC.

Similarly, like a good GPS, a good qualification methodology works hand-in-hand with your sales process.

The qualification method informs the sales rep of their exact location in the sales process and gives instruction on the next steps. It even provides specific details required to move to the next step.

Managing deals on a sales team without an effective qualification methodology tightly synced with your sales process would be like driving to visit your friend in New York without a GPS and map.

You may get to your destination at some point . . . but not with the most efficient route.

Along the journey, you wouldn't know your current location, how far you traveled, the next turn, distance to the next turn, remaining distance to your destination, or approximate time of arrival. You wouldn't be able to tell your friend when you would arrive.

Without an effective deal-qualification methodology, reps can make themselves—and their sales manager—believe forecasted deals are more qualified than they are in reality. That divergence between fairy tale and reality significantly alters the accuracy of your forecast.

The divergence problem increases in severity proportional to the size of your sales organization.

If, at each level of the salesforce, managers lack a common method to qualify the status of a deal, then, without malice, each manager rolls an inaccurate forecast up to the next level. That next level is also incapable of systematically qualifying deals.

The likely result is multiple sales teams missing their respective booking numbers and the entire sales force missing the quarter.

WHAT IS MEDDPICC?

"So that's why we can never dissect a deal during a forecast review," Jim said, eyes bright with an *ah ha!* moment. "We never seem to be able to understand the exact status, let alone what's going right or what's going wrong."

"Yes!"

"I think that's why we barrage the reps with questions during the forecast sessions. We just don't know what to ask. Through a mountain of questions, we're hoping to understand what is happening in the account."

"Does it help?" I asked.

"No. Because we never had a sales process or a way to analyze deals."

"Exactly."

Stevie Mac raised a hand. "Having worked at several companies, why is it that most sales forces don't have a deal-qualification methodology?"

"It's simple. First, they never constructed a step-by-step sales process like the one we reviewed in prior meetings. Second, even if they did have a sales process, they never linked their sales process to their qualification methodology. Something I'm going to show you how to do right now. Let me introduce you to a proven qualification method named MEDDPICC."

MEDDPICC
Metrics
Economic Buyer
Decision Criteria
Decision Process
Identify the Pain or Initiative
Paper Process
Champion
Competition

Andy had a puzzled expression. "I've heard that MEDDPICC is a sales process."

"Nope, that's a common misconception." I stated.

Then I explained that it's a *framework*, which allows you to do the following:

1. **Rapidly identify an opportunity:** You'll be able to quickly understand if the customer is buying what you're selling.
2. **Swiftly acknowledge your location in the sales process:** Know if you entered a deal early or late in the

customer's buying process. Know which stage you are in, the steps you've taken, the people you've met, and the information you've obtained.

3. **Understand the gap between known and unknown:** Recognize the knowns and unknowns. Recognize what information and which people in the sales process are known and unknown.
4. **Build an action plan to get back on track:** Create your logical next steps in the account
5. **Analyze rep knowledge and skills:** Uncover gaps in your rep's ability to perform in the sales process

It's the GPS to your sales process.

"Your sales process happens in chronological order, right?" I asked.

"Right," they said in unison.

"Like a GPS can be utilized at any point during the drive from Boston to New York City, MEDDPICC can be used at any point in the sales process."

Since MEDDPICC is just an acronym, I'm not going to describe MEDDPICC in the order of its letters. I'll walk through MEDDPICC based on how it links seamlessly to the chronological stages of your sales process. We're going to start with Identify since the first stage of your process is Discovery."

47
IDENTIFY THE PAIN, PROBLEM, OR INITIATIVE

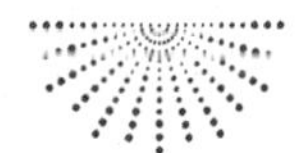

Any deal without an identified pain, problem, or initiative will not have a high priority in any business. Getting *above the noise* to solve a major business pain becomes the driver for purchasing a solution. Attaching your unique differentiators to the solution to that business pain and driving urgency creates a higher business value for your solution.

Those answers lie in the Three WHYs:

1. Why do they have to buy?
2. Why do they have to buy from us?
3. Why do they have to buy now?

WHY DO THEY HAVE TO BUY?

This question uncovers a treasure trove of information, revealing deep insights into two critical components of any deal:

The customer pains.
The buyer most impacted by the pain.

*Why do they **HAVE TO** buy?* divulges whether or not your sales rep *identified* a major pain or a corporate initiative. Their description of the level of the pain is telling. Is the pain above the noise? Is their description in technical or business terms? These questions allow you to understand their level of investigation during the Discovery stage.

*Why do **THEY** have to buy?* relates to the buyer in the organization who is most impacted by the pain. Who "owns" the pain? Whose job position will be most jeopardized by the pain? Can they name the specific person and articulate why they are impacted?

We've discussed how pain points are viewed quite differently as reps move up and down the hierarchy of an organization. The potential value of the deal related to the severity of the pain and level of the person impacted changes as you climb different levels toward the C-suite.

I discovered the power of understanding the ownership of pain, particularly *why do **THEY** have to buy,* when I first sold CAD (Computer Aided Design).

CAD solutions enhanced the productivity of mechanical engineers when they designed products like car engines and laptops. They could visualize the assembly of components for form, fit, function, and other important design factors.

Logically, you would think a CAD salesperson would target the Director of CAD in companies.

You couldn't be more wrong.

Why?

Directors of CAD didn't have to buy. They'd already implemented a CAD solution for the engineers. The CAD director didn't have any personal pain. He didn't use a CAD system and wasn't measured on his ability to design a new product. He went home at 5:00 p.m. without pain.

No one wants to self-inflict pain. The CAD Director was no different.

Why inflict personal pain? Replacing the current CAD system meant having to implement a new CAD solution, retrain all the engineers, and handle any unforeseen issues. A new CAD system would *generate* pain, not eliminate pain!

There was no personal win for the CAD Director.

The CAD Director became skilled in pushing away enthusiastic CAD sales reps. If you sold unique, whiz-bang features and functions, he had a well-practiced objection. He would explain that he was recently informed by his current vendor that they would have the same whiz-bang features in their next release.

This is a "leapfrog" game. You have more features today; my vendor will leapfrog you in six months.

In other words, *go away*.

No extra pain is required.

The person who "owned" the pain was the VP of Engineering. He needed to increase engineering productivity. Get new products out the door quicker for less cost. That was the person a rep needed to target. The VP Engineering was the *they* in *why do **THEY** have to buy*?

They own the pain. They are most impacted by the pain.

If they can make their engineers more productive and get new products out the door for less cost before the competitors, they can grab additional market share. You've helped them positively impact their business.

A significant *gain over the pain* for the business.

A personal win.

In return, they'll pay a premium for the business value of your solution.

To reiterate, *why do **THEY** have to buy*? reveals whether or not your rep identified the pain and the associated buyer most impacted by the pain during the Discovery stage.

"I agree," Andy said. "We've also seen that deals without the implication of a high degree of pain fizzle out because we haven't found a direct link between the pain and a person, so no one makes it a priority to solve the problem. Remember the Thomson deal was originally forecasted two quarters ago for $200,000, last quarter for $150,000, and this quarter for $100,000. It's going to fizzle out."

They had it exactly right.

WHY DO THEY HAVE TO BUY FROM US?

A second powerful qualifier is: *Why does the customer have to **BUY FROM US**?*

This question is *the beginning of formulating the decision criteria*. When reps can explain the customer pain and alignment to your product differentiators, they have qualified a key element in the Discovery stage: the potential buying criteria.

Your product differentiators need to map directly to the customer's pain points to give you an edge over the competition. It answers the simple question:

Is the customer buying what we're selling?

Customers only care about how your product uniquely solves pains in their specific use case. Nothing else. The SaaS market is full of products with differentiated features which are *nice to have*, not a *need to have*. The solution may be differentiated, but the capabilities don't solve significant pain points in customer-use cases. That leaves the customer without a compelling reason to buy.

If reps can't explain how your product uniquely solves pain in the customer's use case, then the rep hasn't completed the Discovery stage.

If you move past Discovery without identifying why the customer has to buy from you, chances are the customer will believe you and your product are ordinary and indifferent.

Just another indistinguishable product.

Just another indistinguishable sales rep.

WHY DO I HAVE TO BUY NOW?

The third question qualifies whether the rep understands the implications of the customer *not* solving their pain:

Why do I have to buy it ***NOW?***

Reps have to understand this in order to understand customers priorities and drive customer urgency.

Like the story about Dan, who sold me life insurance, the negative consequences change the customer's priorities. It showcases the negative state they are in and display the positive future state. If they don't buy, the consequences of not purchasing the solution are substantial.

What critical business measure suffers by not solving the pain?

The answer to this question reveals the rep's *grasp of the pain's effect* on the customer's business operations *and* discloses the *level of impact* the pain has on the company as a whole. The answer indicates whether or not your product will solve major business pains or low-level pains and is an additional indicator of the level of buyer your rep is speaking with in the account.

For instance, what's the cost of presenting a new gaming application to the holiday market two months late? Which of these will be most affected, product development cost overruns, loss of market share, negative influence on revenues, or profitability?

"So, let me hear it from you," I said, and tossed the marker to Carlos. "Let's build a list of qualifying questions to ask reps based on the Three WHYs in our *Identify* stage that indicate progress during the Discovery stage."

QUALIFYING REPS ON THE 3 WHYS

Why do they HAVE TO buy?

1. How would they describe the level pain level?
2. What are the specific pain points?
3. Is the pain above the noise?
4. Is their description of pain in technical terms, business terms or both?
5. What is the customer use case?

Why do THEY have to buy?

1. Who is most impacted by the pain?
2. What is the title of the person most impacted?
3. How does this pain effect their job measures?

Why do they have to buy from US?

1. Do our product differentiators tie to their pains?
2. Which of our product capabilities is uniquely differentiated?

Why do they have to buy NOW?

1. What happens if they do nothing?
2. What company measurement suffers?
3. Do they have another alternative to solve the pain?
4. Do you know their desired business outcome?

"Just to confirm, when we are qualifying a deal, if our reps can't explain the Three WHYs, then they are still in the Discovery phase?" asked Andy.

"That's absolutely correct. They have to document the pain to understand whether or not the customer has the potential to buy what you're selling and an urgency to solve the problem."

48

METRICS: THE QUANTIFICATION OF PAIN AND THE SOLUTION

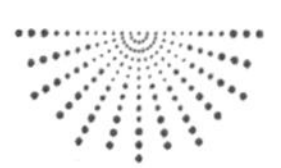

"Let's discuss Metrics, since the next stage in your sales process is Scoping." I gestured to the group. "What do we mean by Metrics?"

"The quantified customer pain," Andy said.

"And the quantification of the business benefits of your solution," Jim added. Andy glanced at him, then nodded in approval. Jim continued. "It qualifies whether or not our reps have an understanding of the before and after scenarios. For example, it previously took twelve months to accomplish a task with five people, each with an annual burden cost of $300,000. After our solution, it will only take two people three months to achieve."

"Good one." Andy nodded. "The rep's ability to describe the before (*as-is*) and after (*to-be*) scenarios is a qualifying indicator of whether or not they performed the Scoping stage, right?"

"Right, Andy," I said. "Without quantifying before and after, your rep cannot build a cost justification that proves tangible business value. A powerful cost justification gives your rep strength later in the process."

The *cost justification sets the price anchor* with the Economic Buyer. Later, that price anchor will give your rep strength when Procurement starts to negotiate price.

Without quantifying value, you're leaving it up to the customer to determine the perceived value of your product and the price they're willing to pay for that value.

Qualifying Reps on Metrics:

Several questions can indicate progress during the Scoping stage:

- What is the use case?
- Who owns the use case?
- How much is the quantified pain?
- Have you outlined the current *as-is* and the desired *to-be* scenarios?
- What is the quantified business value?
- Does the gain far outweigh the pain?
- What is their desired business outcome?
- How do you measure a successful business outcome?
- Do you have current KPIs you track for the business outcome?
- Have you built a preliminary cost justification?
- Have you shared the findings with your Champion?
- Is your Champion in agreement with each element of the justification?
- Have you reconfirmed why they need our differentiators in the *to-be* solution?
- What price point will you set during your meeting with the EB?

"This seems straightforward enough for qualification. Meaning, if our people haven't been able to build the current and desired states with metrics, then they are still in the Scoping stage, right?" asked Luca.

"Correct, Luca."

49
DECISION CRITERIA

The Decision Criteria is the buyer's shopping list, which is formulated in the Discovery stage and documented and finalized in the Scoping stage.

The decision criteria clearly states the *required capabilities that must be in the solution to solve the pain*. The required capabilities define the customer's future state. All competitors will be judged during the decision process and validation event on these criteria.

"But remember, we need to go further to absolutely ensure the customer is buying what you're selling," I said. "How do you do that?"

"If your differentiators are in the final decision criteria, they're buying what you're selling," Hannlin said. "If it's your competitor's differentiators, then they're not buying what you're selling."

Andy inserted, "*Our differentiators must be documented in the final-decision criteria*. That's confirmation of the '*why do they have to buy from us'* question, which we started to formulate in Discovery."

"The rep who helps their Champion write the decision criteria *gains control* over the deal," Carlos said with his usual winning smile. "Remember the story of the $1,000 sports competition at the high school? You can only win if the rules are in your favor."

You have to control the criteria to control the deal.

Qualifying a rep's intimate knowledge of the criteria (and if that criteria is in writing) is an indicator of the rep's ability to find a Champion during the Scoping stage. A Champion will help your rep control the decision criteria.

You can tell if your rep is gaining or losing control by monitoring specific changes to the decision criteria:

If changes to the criteria are in your favor, you're in control or gaining control.

If changes are in the competition's favor, you've lost or are losing control.

"All right," I called, and tossed the marker to Jim. "Write down qualifying questions that reveal an understanding and control of the decision criteria. The answers will also indicate progress in the Scoping stage."

Qualifying Reps on Decision Criteria

We created a list of qualifying decision criteria questions:

- Do your product capabilities align to the customer pains?
- Can you describe their major pain and how our product alleviates that pain?
- Did you help your Champion write the decision criteria?

- Which of our unique product differentiators are in the decision criteria?
- Have the criteria changed since the original agreement?
- If the criteria changed, which competitor has been influencing the criteria?
- What specific differentiators of the competition have been inserted into the criteria?
- When were their differentiators inserted into the criteria?
- Who is the competition speaking with that has the power to change the criteria?
- Are you in control of this deal or is the competition taking control?
- Why do you think you are in control?
- Are you prepared to discuss with the EB how the solution capabilities solve the customer's business pain?

"The entire process from formulation to finalization of the decision criteria is extremely telling. It tells us everything we need to know about our position in the sales process:

- Whether we entered early or late into the sales process
- Where we are in the sales process
- How much power our Champion has
- If we have a coach or a Champion
- How much power the competition's Champion has
- If we have confirmed agreement with the EB

"It also tells us our rep's overall intimacy with the deal." Said Stevie Mac

"Well said, Steve."

50
DECISION PROCESS

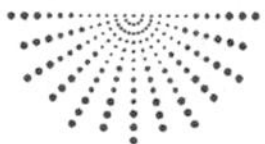

EVALUATE PRODUCTS AND SELECT A SOLUTION

"Anyone want to define the decision process, which is also developed during the Scoping stage?" I asked.

At this point, they were almost carrying it themselves. As if I could see all the pieces coming together in their brain.

"The decision process is the *specific people, events, and time-frames the customer will use to evaluate several products and select a solution*," Hannlin said.

A decision process may look like this:

- Have three vendors perform solution overview presentations by May 1
- Have product demonstrations by May 8
- Create a proof of concept completed by May 15
- Deliver cost justifications by May 22
- Have vendor selection and negotiations finalized by May 29

You have to know who the stakeholders are for each of those events, and you should always validate the decision process with all the people in the process.

"Give me some qualifying questions on decision process," I said and handed the marker to Andy. "I want them to indicate progress during the Scoping stage."

Qualifying Reps on Decision Process

Here are some examples of qualifying decision process questions:

- What are the specific events the company will use to evaluate a solution?
- Besides your Champion, who else will be involved in each event of the decision process?
- Of those people involved in the process, who have you met with one on one?
- Have any new people entered the process since it was created?
- What are the timeframes associated with each event?
- Has the decision process changed since it was first created?
- Who changed it?
- Were you or your Champion involved?
- Is your Champion helping you control the process?
- If not, which competitor's Champion is controlling the process?
- What is the title of the competition's Champion?
- Does the POV have defined start and end dates?
- Which competitors are involved in the process?
- Are you prepared to confirm the decision process with the Economic Buyer?
- Can we meet with the EB after the POV?

Luca summarized the additional qualifying information gained through the decision process:

- The person controlling the process
- Other key stakeholders involved in the process
- The power of the rep's Champion and the power of the competitor's Champion
- Whether or not the remaining steps are predictable or unknown
- Timeframes associated with events
- Our rep's overall intimacy with the deal

51
CHAMPIONS

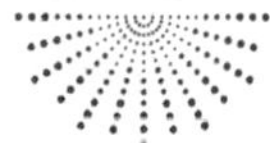

DEAL CONTROL

"Luca, remind everyone of the definition of a Champion."

"The Champion has influence (power) in an account which gives them access to the EB. We're looking for INA's and IA's." said Luca.

There are three big reasons you need a Champion:

1. To gain access to the EB
2. To have an internal salesperson working on our behalf.
3. To gain control of the deal

WHO CONTROLS THE DEAL?

"What is control?" I asked.

"Control defines whether or not we are taking a bus ride, hitching an Uber ride, or driving ourselves during the sales process. Hop on a bus, and you're taking the route and destination defined by the bus company. No control. Hop into an Uber, and the driver takes you the destination, but not the route you define. Some control. Drive yourself, and you define the route and the destination. That's control," said Andy.

"So, how do you qualify *who is in control of the deal?"* I asked. "There can only be one of three parties that can control or gain control of a deal." I displayed three fingers and stared the managers and reps down. "So, which are the three parties that could be in control?

"There's no doubt," Stevie Mac said. "The customer is always in control."

"Stevie, I'm not sure that's true," Jim said with a shake of his head. "I've seen accounts where it seems our competitor is in control. Not the customer."

Andy scoffed. "We certainly aren't in control of most of our accounts. If we were in control, we'd have the confidence to forecast the deal."

"Wait. How is it that the customer isn't in control if they are the ones with the money?" Luca asked. "I'm with Stevie Mac."

Andy raised his hand. "Well, the only way for us to be in control is to have a Champion."

"True," Jim said. "Coaches don't have influence, so they can't help us with control. I think one of the three is the Champion."

"All of those are likely," I said. "But at points during the sales process, things change. Momentum shifts. The flow of information changes. Control is relinquished. Let's take a scenario where competing reps all entered an account at the same time. It makes sense that the customer controls the early stages of the sales process, right?"

A triumphant Luca and Stevie Mac said, "Right!"

They paused so I gave them the answer:

The customer
The competition
You

WHEN THE CUSTOMER IS IN CONTROL

Early in the process, a rep needs to discover a bundle of information from the customer. Even though the customer may not understand the magnitude of their company pain, and they certainly don't understand the value of your product, the *customer is in control, because reps need information from the customer.*

As the sale process progresses into later stages, an information shift naturally occurs. And good sales reps start to take control.

"Why do you think that is?" I asked.

"If the rep slowed down during Discovery and Scoping, and conducted an excellent investigation, they should have a substantial amount of information from thc customer," said Jim.

"They also know the answers to the Three WHYs," Andy interjected.

"And the more information regarding pain they discovered "above the noise," the higher the likelihood they will find a Champion," Carlos added.

"Exactly."

WHEN THE REP IS IN CONTROL

In the later stages of Scoping, the *Champion now needs information from the rep* to sell the deal internally. Things like how to evaluate the product, understand the competition, obtain customer references, and justify the purchase. The information flow is from the rep to the customer.

The rep starts to take control of the deal.

Once good reps gain control with their Champion, they don't relinquish it. They continue to collaborate with the Champion and spread wide and high throughout the account. They find multiple Champions high and low and try to build a groundswell of support.

During any forecast review, when a deal is at the mid-stages of the sales process, qualify whether or not your rep is in control. If they are in control, they should have a Champion. Together with their Champion, they should've created the decision criteria, formulated the decision process, and set a meeting with the Economic Buyer.

The interactions with the account have moved from *unpredictable* to *predictable*. From out of control to in control.

On the flip side, if your rep doesn't have a Champion and can't describe the decision criteria and process in detail, the rep is still in the Scoping stage and not in control.

WHEN THE COMPETITION IS IN CONTROL

If the deal you are reviewing is in Scoping, and the decision criteria and process elements have been defined without your rep, the information may still flow from the prospect to your rep.

But the prospect is usually being controlled by the competition, and your rep is being *told* the criteria and process.

Your rep either entered the deal late, and the competition had a strong Champion, who is helping to control the criteria, the process, and, in turn, your rep. Or your rep entered the deal at the same time as the competition, but the competitor had a Champion, and your rep doesn't.

In both cases, qualify whether or not the competition has a true Champion or a coach. Pay attention to the details of their explanation to *determine who is in control*, which direction information is flowing, and the reps' intimacy with the creation of the decision criteria and process.

Qualifying Reps on Having a Champion.

These questions help to determine whether or not your rep has a Champion and is in control (which would indicate successful Discovery and Scoping stages):

1. Were you told the criteria and process, or did you develop it?
2. Did the Champion help the rep develop what was needed?
3. Before-and-after scenarios
4. Cost justification
5. Decision criteria with your differentiator
6. Decision process
7. Agenda for the EB meeting
8. What is the position of the Champion on the power chart?
9. If they are an IA, how do you know they have influence?
10. If they are an INA, why do they have influence?
11. Are they NINA or ANI?

12. Have you confirmed your Champion has influence with others?
13. What is the Champion's personal win?
14. How have you educated and developed the Champion?
15. How have you tested your Champion?
16. What have they done to make you believe they are a Champion?
17. Who does your Champion say is the Economic Buyer?
18. Has your Champion scheduled a meeting for you with the Economic Buyer?
19. Schedule a prep call for the manager and rep with the Champion prior to the EB meeting

"Would you say your preference is to have the sales leader on a prep call with the rep and the Champion prior to the EB meeting?" asked Stevie Mac.

"Yes, definitely. A good example is when Jim was in the Champion meeting to support Kathleen when she tested and verified her Champion during her prep call at UPS?"

52
ECONOMIC BUYER

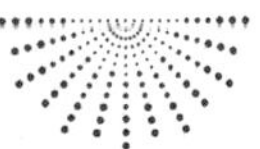

"Jim," I called. "Remind everyone of the definition of an Economic Buyer."

"*The Economic Buyer is the person with the discretionary use of the funds.* That means the Economic Buyer can reallocate the budget. When the Economic Buyer approves, all other signatures are simply rubber stamps."

"How is the Economic Buyer a qualifier?" I asked.

"When selling to a new company, we have to confirm with the Economic Buyer the priority to solve their pain and their willingness to reallocate budget," Andy said. "The EB meeting qualifies that we are selling what they are buying and that the EB has the money and the authority."

"Yes, but you forgot timeframe. During the Economic Buyer meeting, you'll qualify their desired business outcome, their budget, the EBs authority, the priority to solve pain, and the timeframe to purchase."

With the assistance of a Champion, the meeting with the Economic Buyer should be a confirmation meeting, allowing you to verify your findings from the Discovery and Scoping stages. In the meeting, you'll need to confirm the cost justification, decision criteria (validation event criteria, POV criteria), and decision process, and you'll need to obtain purchase approval upon successful completion of the validation event.

QUALIFYING REPS ON EB MEETING PREPARATION

Before the Economic Buyer meeting, you should have answers to the following:

- Who does your Champion say is the Economic Buyer?
- Have you validated the Economic Buyer with multiple people?
- When is the Economic Buyer meeting scheduled?
- What are you prepared to present at the Economic Buyer meeting?
- Has your Champion briefed the Economic Buyer prior to your meeting?

QUALIFYING REPS ON MEETING THE ECONOMIC BUYER

These are questions to ask of your reps who have met the Economic Buyer:

- Did you confirm your Discovery and Scoping findings?
- Did you confirm the Three WHYs?
- Did you confirm the before and after scenarios?
- What is the Economic Buyer's desired business outcome?

- Which Economic Buyer measure is most impacted by the pain?
- Why is this a priority for the Economic Buyer?
- Did the EB agree that all vendors must test to the same validation criteria?
- Can we call the EB if someone tries to change the agreed-upon validation criteria?
- Does the Economic Buyer have authority to make a purchase of this size?
- Did you review the preliminary cost justification with the Economic Buyer?
- Can we meet with the EB if our test results are materially different than our preliminary cost justification?
- Will the Economic Buyer allocate budget, based on your cost justification, to this project?
- In what timeframe does the Economic Buyer want a solution?
- Why does the EB need the solution in the stated timeframe?
- Did you confirm the remaining steps in the decision process?
- Did you gain agreement on a follow-up EB meeting if the results from the validation event materially changed your cost justification?
- What questions did the Economic Buyer ask you?
- What did your Champion say after the meeting?

My preference is for a sales leader to be in every EB meeting to help the sales rep during the meeting and build a relationship with the EB and Champion.

53
COMPETITION

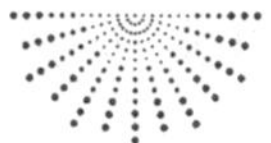

"Your reps should always be concerned, maybe even paranoid, with the movements of their competitors in a forecasted account," I said as I leaned on a table at the front of the room. "They should know which competitor is in the account and which buyer they are meeting. They need to be extremely sensitive to any changes to the decision criteria or decision process. Why?"

"Any changes to the criteria or process may be a red flag," Shannon said.

"Exactly. Changes may indicate that the competition has gained sway in the account, because things are changing in their favor. Someone with power over the criteria is listening to the competitor. It may indicate the competition has developed a Champion, and their Champion may be stronger than your rep's Champion."

In other words, if the decision criteria changes with the competitor's differentiators, you've lost control or are losing control.

The competition has a Champion.

"How do you recognize competitive criteria changes?" I asked.

"First, in order to recognize it, you must be knowledgeable of the strengths of your competitors' products," Luca said. "Know how they position their key differentiators."

Luca continued, "It's important to be intimate with how your competitors sell against you. That will allow you to educate your Champion. Inform them on how to handle competitive traps and typical objections originating from the competition"

"Knowing the competitions' weaknesses," Stevie Mac said, "will help you and your Champion set traps. And you can minimize their strengths by knowing their weaknesses. Create traps, objections, fear, uncertainty, and doubt about their capabilities."

"That's right, Stevie. Remind the group the best way to counter a competitive Champion," I said.

"Ensure that your Champion has more influence than the competitor's Champion. As Carlo said, get *high in the tree* early in the process. The other way to counter a competitive Champion is to find *multiple Champions,* both wide and high in the account to counter a competitor's Champion's influence." answered Stevie Mac.

QUALIFYING REPS ON THE COMPETITION

Several questions can help you understand your rep's knowledge of the competition and control of the account:

- Who is the competition?
- When did they enter the account?
- Were they in the account before us?
- Who is their Champion?
- What is their Champion's influence? (IA or INA)

- Is their Champion stronger than your Champion?
- Have you been able to identify additional competitive Champions?
- Who else is the competition speaking with in the account?
- Have they met the Economic Buyer?
- Was the decision criteria set when you entered the account?
- Did the criteria change to include the competition's differentiators?
- When did the criteria change?
- How is their Champion differentiating their solution?
- How is their Champion strategizing to win?
- Has the decision process changed since the competition entered the account?
- Have you armed your Champion with FUD (fear, uncertainty, and doubt) traps for the competition?
- Is your Champion stronger than the competition's Champion?

54
PAPER PROCESS (OR SIGNATURE/APPROVAL PROCESS)

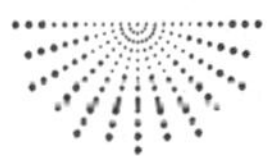

The *paper process* (also known as the signature process or the approval process) *is the step-by-step process the buyer's organization uses to produce a purchase order.* Each step in the process should delineate the people and timeframe involved in processing the paperwork. Knowledge of the time-frame will allow you to forecast accurately.

"Can someone give me an example of a paper process?" I asked.

Andy waved an arm. "I got this. Let's say Joe is your Champion. Joe enters the PR (Purchase Request) and sends it to Francis for financial review, which will take three days. Francis sends it to Marvin for quarterly budgeting process, which will take four days. Then it goes to Larry in Legal for two weeks . . . until it goes to Patty in Procurement, which typically takes two days to issue a purchase order."

I laughed. "Yes. That's it exactly. Without understanding the paper process, it's impossible to accurately forecast. For instance, if there are four weeks left in the quarter and you don't know the paper process is six weeks, you'll definitely miss your forecast."

"If your Champion doesn't know the signature process," Jim said, "it may be an indicator that they aren't a Champion, right?"

"Right."

"Or it's possible they're a first-time Champion: they've never been through the process or bought anything for the dollar amount you've requested. Many times the process changes if the dollar amount exceeds a specified threshold," Hannlin said.

"In that case, you and your Champion need to understand who *has* purchased something for the same dollar amount or higher," Andy said. "Get with that person and map the paper process out so you both know."

"Great idea, Andy," I acknowledged.

Luca said, "It's also important to get contracts from both Legal and Procurement from your Champion. You can introduce your Legal contact to the customer's Legal counsel, and you should immediately introduce yourself to the Procurement person. Knowing those people early will save time in obtaining a purchase order."

QUALIFYING REPS ON THE PAPER (APPROVAL) PROCESS

These questions help you understand where the rep is in the Negotiate and Close stage:

- Does your Champion know the approval process?
- Has your Champion been involved in purchasing a product larger than $X?
- Walk me through the steps in the approval process.

- Who are the stakeholders involved in each of these steps?
- What is the timeframe for each step of the process?
- What is the name of the Legal contact?
- Have our documents been redlined by their Legal?
- Have you spoken to the contact in the Procurement Department?

"Now that we have covered sales process and qualification methodology, I want to make it clear that this is just the science part of sales. There is also the art of the sale. Every salesperson is unique. Every salesperson will interface and communicate with customers in their own style. Every rep may ask questions, respond to objections, build rapport, listen, and use their personality, curiosity, humor and intuition differently. That is the *art* of the sale."

The sales process and qualification method each outline the information needed—the steps to take which people to meet. That's the *science* of the sale.

Every sale is part science and part art.

The clock that ticked away in the back of the room grabbed my attention—not to mention their glassy-eyed expressions. With all of the qualification methodology behind us, now it was time for them to implement.

They had a QBR coming up with their reps. Now they could prepare themselves to ask the *right* questions to help coach their reps and prepare an accurate forecast. I'd follow up with them after the end of the quarter.

"Time to call it for the day," I said, and set the marker in the tray. "Good luck finishing out the quarter strong."

55
QUALIFICATION CONTINUED

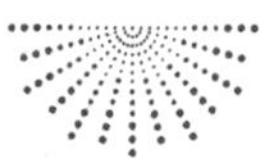

After the end of the quarter, my curiosity almost got the best of me. Still, I waited for the group to tell me the news about the quarter. They were traveling to meet me in Boston.

We met in a conference room at the Mandarin Oriental Hotel in Boston's Back Bay section of the city. The hotel was located on Boylston Street, just steps from the Boston Marathon finish line. Less than one block away from where two pressure-cooker bombs had exploded, killing three and injuring 264 people.

The city seemed fully recovered, as businesses was back to normal. Restaurants and bars had reopened, and pedestrians felt safe walking the Back Bay again. I had bought tickets for the entire group to attend the Boston Bruins–Philadelphia Flyers hockey game that night at the Garden.

Raj called me during my Uber ride to the Mandarin Oriental. "We beat our quarterly number by fifteen percent, John," he said. "It set a record for the number of new logos and increased our average deal size to $95,000. The average productivity per rep jumped to 1.4 million dollars."

"Congratulations! Those are far better numbers."

"I know we're not all the way there yet, because our forecasting ability is still suspect. Our forecast was ten percent off of our finish but ten percent over the original forecast. However, the improvement in our selling and qualifying of accounts is very welcomed. We're making a few changes, based on the results, for the continued consistency I'm seeing in our sales process. With productivity at $1.4M, I've decided to hire more sales reps and scale the sales force."

"Did you promote anyone?" I asked with Jim in mind.

He laughed. "Yes, as a matter of fact, Jim is now an Area Director, and Kathleen has been promoted to sales manager."

"What about Andy?"

"He was disappointed that he didn't get the director job, but he understood. Jim had performed better and has proven to be a better leader over the course of the last year."

Raj was right. Andy hadn't been ready quite yet, but Jim was.

Raj seemed to figuratively wave that off. "I'd predict that Andy will be the next manager to get promoted, then I think Carlos in the US and Luca in Europe will be the next people to be promoted as the sales force scales."

"That's exciting," I said as the Uber driver pulled to a stop.

When I entered the conference room, the group mingled together. I walked over and congratulated Kathleen on her new position.

"Since our training sessions," she said, "I found a way to not only find and build strong Champions, but most of my meetings are now with executives, much *higher up in the tree*. And I closed my biggest deal ever—1.15 million dollars."

"That sounds more like it," I remarked. "How did you do it?"

"As you've told us, *attach to the pain above the noise* and build a powerful cost justification with a high-level Champion. We worked on a business issue that affected a critical corporate measure."

Jim looked over at me and gave me a quick nod and smile, indicating that he knew I knew about his promotion to Area Director. In that glance, I saw his gratitude for what he'd learned.

All progress aside, it was now time for me to help this transforming group with a forecasting strategy.

In other words, our work wasn't done yet.

PART V
FORECASTING STRATEGY

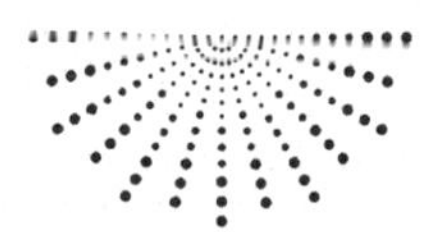

56

FORECASTING

"We'll talk about a few high-level forecasting strategies today, but can someone remind the group what consistent forecasting accuracy indicates?"

Jim answered, "It is a gauge of how intimate we are as sales leaders with our people and the accounts in the forecast."

"Right, Jim," I said. "Your ability to forecast accurately is telling. It tells if you are able to qualify the accounts you've visited with your reps and qualify with your reps on accounts you didn't visit. If you are truly intimate with your rep's selling abilities and have qualified their forecasted accounts, your forecast should be consistently accurate every quarter."

"OK, but some sales leaders forecast poorly one quarter, either because they aren't familiar, or, as you say, intimate with their people and the deals, or because so many deals slipped into the next quarter, leaving forecast is accurate," Andy emphasized with apparent frustration.

"You're right Andy, that's why I said consistently accurate every quarter. Forecast accuracy for one quarter is just a point. Two quarters of accuracy is a line. Three straight quarters is a trend. For Forego to scale the sales force and the business, Raj and Dennis need you to consistently forecast accurately. They need predictability and consistency to the business."

BANT VS. MEDDPICC

Andy anxiously raised his hand, "I'm curious. I've heard of another qualification method named BANT. Stands for Budget, Authority, Need, and Time. How does BANT compare to MEDDPICC?"

"First, BANT is an acronym for:

BUDGET
AUTHORITY
NEED
TIMING

"Second, BANT is very useful and has relevant questions to qualify at the Economic Buyer level," I said.

In the Economic Buyer meeting, you want to confirm all the BANT elements:

1. The Economic Buyer ranks the pain as a priority (NEED) to solve.
2. They want to solve it in a specific timeframe (TIME).
3. The EB has the authority (AUTHORITY) to buy.
4. The EB will allocate budget (BUDGET) for purchase if the validation event is successful.

However, BANT *doesn't mesh seamlessly with your sales process to*:

1. Qualify the *information and people required at each step and stage of the sales process*.
2. Accurately identify tangible deal advancement
3. Help diagnose specific areas where your reps are struggling in accounts.

BANT *doesn't address key stakeholders*:

1. Developing a Champion (C)
2. Identifying and meeting the Economic Buyer (E)
3. Understanding the Competition (C) the competition's Champion (C), and their combined strategy

BANT *doesn't dictate the completion of key selling steps to drive value, forecast accurately and ensure success*:

1. Identify pain, problem or an initiative (I) above the noise
2. Quantify the as-is and to-be metrics (M) into a cost justification
3. Frame the decision criteria (D)
4. Control the decision process (D)
5. Identify the players and steps in the (P) paper process

With MEDDPICC tightly linked to your sales process, you can *quickly identify the knowns and unknowns* in the sales process and build an action plan to get back on track.

Like a good GPS system, MEDDPICC let's you know the exact location in the process, upcoming elements to acheive, and the approximate time to an order for accurate forecasting. MEDDPICC informs you of which stage you are in, the steps you've taken, the people you met, what information you have, and what information you need.

And, unlike BANT, MEDDPICC qualifies the journey from both the customer's perspective *and* the rep's perspective to maximize business value for the customer and order value for the rep.

57
FORECASTING QUALIFICATION STRATEGY

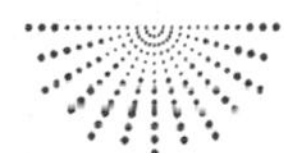

Andy lifted his hand. "You've given us some great tools that are helping us become better forecasters, but in our last QBR I felt a little . . . uncertain. What should our strategy be as managers during and after a forecast session to ensure we forecast accurately?"

"Great question, Andy. First, I always remember the basics":

- Have a common Vocabulary.
- Listen.
- Be HERE.
- Use your intuition.
- Have a transformational mindset.
- Inspire, coach, and inspect.
- Desire a win-win outcome.
- Be self-aware.
- Have urgent curiosity.

PUSH DEALS OFF

If you've exhausted your qualifying questions and, for some reason, your rep can't articulate the exact status of the deal, *push it off the forecast.* Tell the rep you want them to remove it from the forecast.

If you've trained and coached your rep on the sales process and qualifying, the burden of proof should be on your rep to present all the facts and you to probe and qualify the account situation.

That said, there should be preponderance of evidence to keep the deal in the forecast. If there isn't solid evidence of a deal that can close in the quarter, push it of the forecast.

"I don't believe it is a deal for this quarter," you can say. "Take it off the forecast."

"It's always difficult to tell them to take it off the forecast," said Andy.

"I understand, Andy, but it does two things."

1. Naturally, it forces the rep to respond with more account information, which may reveal the evidence you need to feel confident in forecasting.
2. After the deal is removed from the forecast, it typically leaves the rep short of their quota. They're left with a gap. The gap compels the rep to reconcile the difference to their quota. In a reconciliation process, they need to *find another deal* to replace the removed deal and close the gap.

"As a manager," I asked. "What do you have to lose?"

"Nothing. It's a smart strategy, even if it may not make me popular with that rep. If the removed deal winds up being real and the rep finds another deal through the reconciliation process, my forecast grew. If the removed deal winds up not being real, I covered the forecast with a new deal through the reconciliation process. It's a win-win."

"It's a win-win if you also coach your rep on why it is not a qualified deal. Let's talk about the reconciliation process right now," I said.

PEAS AND CARROTS

My son loves to eat.

It's difficult to keep two refrigerators stocked when he's in the house. But when he was young, it was a different story.

At around eight years old, he loved to eat his meat and potatoes during dinner. I'd watch as he'd spread his peas and carrots evenly around the edge of his plate to make it look like he had those as well.

He'd announce, "I'm done."

Then he'd try to excuse himself from the dinner table so he could play with his friends.

"Not so fast," I'd say. "Hold on a second."

On purpose, I'd stare at his plate so he could see me looking at it. Then I would ask, "Are you done?"

Unwavering, he'd answer, "Yes, I'm done."

"It doesn't look like you're done!"

He would look me directly in the eyes and say, "Yes. Yes, I'm done. I'm definitely done."

So, I'd reach over to his plate with my fork and shove all the peas and carrots back into a visible pile of vegetables.

"Now, does it look like you're done?"

He'd sigh and say, "No."

If I let him think he was done when he *wasn't* done, he'd have started to believe that eating just meat and potatoes counted as finishing a meal. I needed to reconcile the difference between what *he* thought constituted a finished meal and the definition of a finished meal.

After I told the story, I explained how it related. "Your job as a sales manager is no different," I said. "When you're qualifying a rep's deals during a forecast session, they will try to convince you that all of their deals are fully qualified. If you believe them, then they believe their job is done.

"Your job is to constantly qualify deals off the forecast early in the quarter, leaving sufficient time to build pipeline and find and close other deals. In other words—push unqualified deals off the forecast. Show there's more work to be done."

RECONCILIATION

In any forecasting session, any shortfall to quota by any rep needs to be reconciled.

For instance, if the total of a rep's forecastable deals is $200,000, but quota for the quarter is $300,000 then, just like my son and his vegetables, they still have work to do.

Often, managers let reps leave unqualified deals on the forecast, even though, as we've seen, they aren't real deals for the quarter.

Why do some managers choose to leave these deals in the forecast?

Because some managers are emotionally persuaded by the rep's insistence that the deal is real. With the manager's OK, the reps leave the session believing that they don't need to do any additional pipeline work to find new deals.

If the manager thinks they are done, they must be done.

Instead, the manager should use the session as a teaching moment. Let the rep know that they are not done.

Teach them why

Coach them on how to qualify appropriately. By working with them on a reconciliation process early in the quarter, you're teaching them how to qualify their own accounts and to reconcile the gap between their forecast's shortfall and the quota.

In most sales organizations, the manager doesn't ask insightful qualifying questions early in the quarter. Therefore, they never manage through a reconciliation process.

The manager waits until the last few weeks of the quarter, when deals start dropping out of the forecast because those deals never should have been forecasted.

Then the manager starts asking insightful, probing qualification questions. But it's too late for this regretful discovery: There's not enough runway left in the quarter. Now the manager is stuck with the stress and fear of missing their forecasted number.

RECONCILIATION LESSON

The first time I faced a forecast shortfall, I learned my reconciliation lesson.

It happened on the first week of the quarter. After being out on sales calls all day, I returned to my office around 6:00 p.m. After resolving a few issues, I reviewed the initial forecast rollup from my team. I was shocked to see the rollup be a one-million-dollar deficit from my quota for the quarter.

At 7:00 p.m., I walked out of my office to question a few of the reps about the forecast. Everyone had gone home. I had an empty feeling in my stomach . . . like I was left alone by the team.

Why was I the only remaining person in the office?

Was I the only one who cared about the forecast?

It made me wonder if the reps truly cared as much as I did. My quota for the quarter was $300,000 per rep. Multiplied by seven reps, that's 2.1 million dollars. The forecasts from the sales team rolled up to only 1.1 million dollars. It seemed like my team dropped a one-million-dollar bomb on my desk and left me with the sole responsibility to close the abyss.

There was no way for me to find one million dollars in the next eighty-five days.

At first, I felt angry and pissed off. Like most first-time sales managers, I wanted to yell at my sales team and demand that they increase their forecasts. But as I calmed down on the drive home, I thought that I should cajole and intimidate the reps. Then they'd commit to a higher number for the quarter.

But just because they committed to a higher forecast number, didn't mean the deals they'd forecasted would close.

I'd get a temporary relief because they'd commit to a higher number, but the reality would hit me later in the quarter, when those same deals would fall out of the forecast.

Once home, I grabbed a beer out of the refrigerator and sat down. It dawned on me that I shouldn't shoulder the entire burden of the one-million-dollar shortfall. This was a team. If I carried the entire burden myself, only I would suffer.

I'd be stressed for eleven weeks, while my reps would carry on throughout the quarter without a worry. With me bearing the load, it would never teach my team how to avoid a low forecast in the future.

FORECAST RECONCILIATION

Faced with the one-million-dollar shortfall and needing a line of sight to the quarterly number, I gathered the team together the next day and asked each rep to perform a forecast reconciliation.

The forecast reconciliation for a rep might look something like this:

Quarterly Quota: $300,000

Closed & Committed: $200,000

Forecasted Shortfall: $100,000

Forecasted Reconciliation Target (4x Forecast Gap): $400,000

The forecast-reconciliation target should be at least four times the amount of their gap, to ensure that they find $100,000 before the end of the quarter. Just reconciling to $100,000 was sure to fail, since the probability to close every deal was low.

Assuming a 25-percent probability to close, the rep had to build a plan for $400,000.

Building a $400,000 plan to cover a $100,000 shortfall was a *painful* learning moment.

But sometimes learning comes in the pain of understanding. Understanding that, weeks earlier, it would have been easier to build a pipeline with $100,000 of qualified deals than to try to find $400,000 within the current quarter.

The Forecast Reconciliation will look something like this: (Where the rep was tracking deals based on their qualified stage in the sales process.)

	Discovery	Scope	EB	Validate Event	Bus.Case	N&C
Account #1		$75K				
Account #2			$20K			
Account #3					$40K	
Account #4		$50K				
Account #5	$50K					
Account #6		$70K				
Account #7				$80K		
Account #8	$25K					
Account #9			$30K			
Totals	$75K	$100K	$50K	$80K		

Forecast reconciliation by Stage

Next, for each account, the rep wrote the specific activity they would perform to close that deal amount.

Account	Activity
Account #1	Hold firm on current price during negotiations to increase deal size.
Account #2	Discuss with Economic Buyer at Account #2 to accelerate purchase of Q4 deal.
Account #3	Increase deal size by accelerating additional Q4 licenses with a discount.
Account #4	Dig deeper during Scope with champion at Account #4 to uncover additional pain to drive deal urgency.
Account #5	Find a $50,000 deal with channel partner XYZ at Account #5.
Account #6	Discuss accelerating deal at Account # 6 with champion.
Account #7	Drive an additional $80,000 of value during Validation Event at Account #7 to put in Business Case.
Account #8	Find $25,000 in Installed Base Account #8 for their upcoming project.
Account #9	Ask the Economic Buyer at Account #9 to add additional licenses to Q3 purchase for deeper discount.

Forecast Reconciliation by Account

The forecast reconciliation process spread the pain and the burden of the forecast shortfall across all members of my sales team. It also made them realize that their forecast shortfall was due to their lack of consistent pipeline generation and an inability to effectively qualify deals on their forecast.

If we assume that reps have a sales process to follow and understand how to sell and qualify, then low forecasts are always due to low pipeline activity.

PIPELINE

"You've mentioned pipeline a few times," Andy said. "I think the reason many reps have a weak forecast is because they don't have a big enough pipeline, so they clutch onto deals they hope will close while trying to get us to believe they're real deals."

"That's right, Andy," I said. "Most times, they grasp onto accounts that may have little to no chance to buy. And, during the forecast sessions, they will try to convince you that there is a possibility that the account with close. That's why it's best to qualify those deals off their forecast, which allows them to concentrate on quality opportunities and forces them to generate a pipeline of additional qualified deals."

Pipeline is the lifeblood of a rep.

It's oxygen. Without pipeline, no rep will last long. Every manager with a sales cycle of ninety days or greater knows that not having enough qualified deals entering the quarter means a quarter of the extreme pain and stress of trying to find new deals in the quarter.

The stress of trying to invent deals with existing customers or push new clients to buy prematurely is not a way to endear yourself with current or potential customers.

We know what happens when you try to invent deals or push clients to buy: you end up vending.

You don't have enough time to sell. You skip steps in your sales process to make something happen. You end up discounting to get deals in the timeframe of your quarter, not in the natural timeframe of a customer's value-based evaluation process.

And in this process of inventing deals, you embed yourself and your sales team into a horrific culture. You strain your sales team by constantly coaxing, cajoling, and pushing them to do more.

They live in a hot box.

Every day you push them to find new pipeline deals, expand the size of deals on the current forecast, and return to existing customers to get an order prematurely. A premature order at a sizeable discount.

That's just stealing from the future.

And, of course, without a large pipeline and enough forecastable deals, you also live in a pressure cooker. Carrying the stress of impending doom at the end of the quarter, when you miss your number and have to answer to your manager. You try to deflect their scrutiny with excuses; last minute excuses as to why the customer couldn't buy this quarter but will buy next quarter.

PIPELINE IS HARD WORK

So, why don't sales managers pay close attention to pipeline generation every week to ensure they have created enough qualified pipeline deals for the next quarter?

Because building pipeline every week is painstaking hard work.

It's hard work for the manager to help reps create new pipeline and to diligently inspect weekly pipeline generation activities. It is difficult to consistently hold reps accountable week in and week out.

For the reps, it requires discipline. It's tireless work to cold call, email, network through partners, connect socially, follow up on leads, qualify lead lists, and MQLs.

The persistent effort, the constant diligence and accountability to filling the pipeline, is the only way to ensure that your team has enough deals to make next quarter's number.

As Mike Tyson said, "Discipline is doing what you hate to do but doing it like you love it."

A HUGE PIPELINE MASKS ALL PROBLEMS

On the flip side, a huge pipeline masks all sales issues.

Several times, I was lucky enough to have Jeremy run European sales. Jeremy is a Brit with the self-given nickname—The

Ginger Prince. Jeremy is super smart, with great sense of humor. He's highly competitive, has great intuition, and is a ball of perpetual energy.

He uses those characteristics to always lead from the front and be a role model for his team. Super-fast on his feet, Jeremy always has a quick wit and an insightful, humor-filled response. He delivers his response to any verbal jab or attack as he looks you in the eyes, like a Cheshire Cat, with a wide, ear-to-ear grin.

His guiding principle was the power of possessing a large pipeline of qualified deals. Jeremy knew that selling and qualifying without a large pipeline meant a quarter of anxiety and intolerable pain. Because of his dedication to pipeline generation, I can't ever remember him missing a quarterly number in the many years and multiple companies we worked together.

Jeremy's nickname should have been The Pipeline-Generation King. After congratulating Jeremy at the end of every quarter on his over-quota performance, I used to tell the PG King that I knew he had issues with his team.

Selling and qualification issues.

But I had extreme difficulty finding those issues because his qualified pipeline was always so big, it masked all of his issues.

The Ginger Prince would just look me in the eyes and give me his Cheshire-Cat grin. He knew he had issues . . . but he wasn't allowing me to find them. And he had the confidence to know I would never find those issues if he continued to be The Pipeline-Generation King.

TAKE ME TO YOUR CHAMPION

"OK, let me recap," Jim said. "We keep the qualification basics in mind, qualify deals using MEDDPICC, then push uncertain deals off the forecast. If there is a shortfall, we perform a reconciliation process. Anything else?"

"Yes—you're not done yet. If you want to truly understand the quality of your forecast, then after the forecast session, you'll need to further verify whether or not the remaining deals on the forecast are absolutely qualified.

"The most efficient way to understand those accounts is to ask your reps to, 'Take me to your Champion.'

"You'll want to *meet with the Champion for each of the forecasted deals* to ensure your rep has a Champion and is in control."

Maniacally qualifying deals early in the quarter by visiting the Champions of your reps' forecasted deals *in the first month* of a quarter is one of the surest methods of gaining a deep understanding of your forecast.

Previously you pushed many deals off the forecast. Now, with eleven to twelve weeks to go in the quarter, you've left enough time for your reps to generate new pipeline deals and work other existing customer deals.

After meeting with the Champions of all the forecasted deals in the first month of the quarter, you'll have time during the remainder of the quarter to visit the newly generated deals from the forecast reconciliation.

"Make sense?" I asked.

Jim gave me a thumbs up.

TRANSFORMED

Something told me they've been transformed. I knew it and they felt it. That's when I looked at all the now-familiar faces in the room. They'd done it. They had arrived. They had a functioning sales process. Their managers had a common vocabulary, and they had learned to qualify deals, identify pain above the noise, find and develop Champions high in the tree, sell business value, understand business outcomes, identify red flags, win POVs, coach their people on knowledge and skill issues, and take ownership of their leadership positions.

They learned the basics. They adapted and focused on the essential elements of leadership and selling. They were on their way to mastering the fundamentals.

Simplicity becomes a limitless gift presented to individuals that master the fundamentals.

The effects had already rippled through the company and showed in their sales performance and confident expressions.

"Any questions?" I asked.

This time, no one raised a hand.

They only see light.

There is no more darkness.

They don't need me anymore.

"I can't tell you how proud I am to have watched the transformation of this team. When I first arrived, you were a group of glorified scorekeepers, mismanaging a QBR forecast session with no common vocabulary, no sales process, and no method for you to analyze your deals or coach your people.

"Since that time, I've watched as you've grown from a feature-function sales force, selling small-dollar deals at low levels in accounts to a value-based sales team selling large dollar deals to business Champions and EBs in accounts.

"More importantly, you and your people are able to quickly qualify which accounts to spend your time on, to assess what is going right or wrong in an account, and to acknowledge the next logical steps to get deals back on track.

"And for Forego, it means a continual expansion of the sales force. That growth equates to people growing as individuals, earning more, learning more, and participating in future promotions. A complete and total transformation.

"I'm truly proud of you and inspired by your desire to change."

A NEW FUTURE

Before the Boston Bruins game started, we all took the T (Boston's subway) from the Back Bay Station down to North Station and up into Banners, a new restaurant attached to the Garden. The group was in a celebratory mood. They looked—and acted—much more like a cohesive team than the set of individuals I'd met many months ago.

After dinner, we entered the Garden and I sat next to Jim and Andy waiting for the Bruins game to start. We enjoyed the cool smell of the air and anticipation of the puck drop and game time excitement.

"Are you disappointed that you didn't get promoted?" I asked Andy.

A flicker of something—maybe amusement—went through his gaze. "Nah, I get it. We're all the same in that we all believe we're so different. But I've learned that Jim and I have much more in common. Jim is the better leader. I've learned a lot from watching him lead and manage his team, and I'm figuring out where I need to change." A wry expression crossed his face here.

"I was a one-trick pony, and I learned that I can't muscle my way through sales that require new skills."

I laughed. His expression sobered.

"Listen, John, thanks for helping me change. I didn't realize I'd been such a difficult and stubborn leader. You changed me as a sales leader, but the changes I made as a leader also changed my life."

"Really?" I asked. "How?"

There was a trace of renewed confidence in his eyes when he said, "I moved my family out of a townhome in Southie and into the MetroWest suburbs. I left my old world behind, and I have hope that I can build a different life for me and my family." He shrugged slightly. "I've been punished by the lies I told myself. I've always believed that I was different. Standing on the wrong side of the road as everyone went in a different direction. I now see myself and the world differently. Now I see *myself* as my biggest competitor, not the other managers, not anyone else. The only way I'm going to be a great leader and get what I want is to change myself." He laughed.

Then he continued, "My new motto is, 'help enough people get what they want, and I'll get what I want.' That goes for my team *and* my customers."

"That sounds perfect, Andy."

While he excused himself to grab a round of beers, Jim leaned over. "Hey, John, I just wanted to thank you."

"You did great work, Jim."

"In many ways, I instinctively understood there was a better way to sell and manage. Just like any sport, I *knew* there had to be a playbook and an effective way to analyze accounts and coach my reps, too. But the way I was taught to sell was through sheer activity, and that became the only way I knew to manage." He shook his head. "As you say, I was nothing more than a glorified scorekeeper. The change was . . . hard. But now I'm so thankful that I learned how to coach. That was huge. You've given me an opportunity to lead again, just like in my hockey days. Being a captain of a hockey team gave me a head start over the other managers, so I'm confident in my new role as Area Director. So . . . thank you."

Things changed for us that March night.

It was the last night I would see this group for well over a year. It was the last night the sales leaders would be unsure of the fundamentals. It was also the last night that the sales this sales force would ever feel uncomfortable or out of control in a sales situation.

Their lives and their careers had been changed forever.

ABOUT THE AUTHOR

John McMahon is widely recognized as the only person having been the CRO (Chief Revenue Officer) at five public, enterprise software companies, PTC, Geo-Tel, Ariba, BladeLogic and BMC.

John's expertise was formulated as a pre-IPO member of 4 of the 5 companies listed above.

Today, John is a board member at public software companies Snowflake, MongoDB and private, pre-IPO companies Lacework, Sigma, Cybereason and Observe. In the past, John has been a board member and executive consultant to: Hubspot, Glass Door, AppDynamics and Sprinklr.

ACKNOWLEDGMENT

Big thanks to Katie Cross for being an incredible coach